BOMBERS OF WWII

JEFFREY L. ETHELL

Lowe & B. Hould
Publishers

This edition published in 2001 by Lowe & B. Hould Publishers, an imprint of Borders, Inc., 515 East Liberty, Ann Arbor, MI 48104. Lowe & B. Hould Publishers is a trademark of Borders Properties, Inc.

Previously published in 1994 by MBI Publishing Company, Galtier Plaza, Suite 200, 380 Jackson Street, St. Paul, MN 55101-3885 USA

© Jeffrey L. Ethell, 1994

Library of Congress Cataloging-in-Publication Data Available

ISBN 0-681-60722-X

Pinted in Hong Kong

On the front cover: An 18thSquadron, 34th Bomb Group B-17G sits out an approaching storm while visiting Mt. Farm. *Robert Astrella*

On the frontispiece: Copilot Lieutenant William C. Rowland from New Castle, Pennsylvania, off to war from England in a B-24. Relationships on the flight deck could be good, could be bad. A great deal depended upon the attitude of the aircraft commander in the left seat. Some gae their copilots half of the flying time, while others were of the "gear up, flaps up, shut up" variety. *USAF*

On the title page: A flight of 352nd Fighter Group Mustangs, the "Blue Nose Bastards of Bodney," shepherd 458th Bomb Group Liberators across the English Channel, mid–1944. *USAF*

On the back cover: Top: B-17Fs of the 401st Squadron, 91st Bomb Group, low over England in early 1943. Based at Bassingbourn, the 91st was one of the pioneer Eighth Air Force heavy bomb groups, the first to attack a target in the Ruhr-Hamm area on 4 March 1943. Without extensive fighter escort through that year, the going was rough indeed. *USAF* Bottom: When *5 Grand* (the 5,000th B-17 built by Boeing) went to war, it carried the company employees' autographs all the way to the 96th Bomb Group at Snetterton Heath. Here the B-17 makes a shakedown flight over England before getting painted with the group identification letter (square C), individual call letter (H), red vertical fin stripes on the tail, and squadron codes (BX) on the fuselage. *5 Grand* must have been a lucky ship; after seventy-eight missions, it went home to end up in t scrap yard. *USAF*

Contents

Introduction

At its height in World War II, the US Army Air Forces had 2,411,294 men and women in uniform. By the time the war was over, the Army Air Forces would take delivery of almost 230,000 aircraft to be flown by 193,440 pilots. By far the majority of the Army Air Forces' effort went into manning the service's bombers, the very heart of American air power doctrine. The numbers built of each type were staggering: 12,677 B-17s at $204,370 each in 1944; 18,188 B-24s (more than any single American aircraft in history) for $215,515 each; 9,815 B-25s at $142,194 each; 5,157 B-26s at $192,427 each; 3,760 B-29s for $605,360 each; 7,230 A-20s at $100,800 each; and 2,446 A-26s at $192,457 each.

Between Pearl Harbor and VJ-Day, the army aircrew training machine used 475 facilities, 30,000 aircraft, and a million people to train 497,533 aircraft and engine mechanics, 347,236 gunners, 195,422 radio mechanics and operators, 50,976 navigators, 47,354 bombardiers, and 193,440 pilots. Between December 1942 and August 1945, most of these personnel ended up in or worked on a bomber. Over 29,350 heavy bombardment crews were formed, and 7,600 medium and light bomber crews were created.

The army gave these men a base pay, to which could be added flying pay and foreign-service pay. In 1945 a technical sergeant made $114 a month; with flying pay added, that went up to $171. Total pay for service overseas came to $193.80 a month. A captain earned $200 per month; if he flew, his pay climbed to $300. On foreign service, the total could be $320.

Of all the combat jobs in the American services during World War II, from infantryman to submariner, no job was more dangerous, statistically, than that of a man in a bomber over Germany. The Eighth and Fifteenth Air Forces took a higher percentage of losses than any other American fighting force, from foxhole to destroyer deck. Though the glamour of the Army Air Corps (as it continued to be known regard-

Two red flares arc up from a 381st Bomb Group B-17 on short final at Ridgewell— wounded aboard! The Dodge "meat wagon" was a standard fixture at all Eighth Air Force fields. A bomb group usually had more than one on hand at the end of a mission. *USAF*

less of the name change in 1941) seemed to shine throughout the war, the air war was not clean or safe. It was murderous.

Flying 264,618 bomber and 257,321 fighter sorties from England, the Eighth Air Force lost 4,148 B-17s and B-24s; 2,042 fighters were also lost, with 43,742 airmen killed or missing and another 1,923 seriously wounded. The Fifteenth Air Force flew 148,955 bomber and 87,732 fighter sorties out of Italy, losing a proportionate number of men. Once transferred from the Mediterranean, the Ninth Air Force, though mostly a fighter air force, flew 368,500 sorties to lose 2,139 fighters and 805 bombers (and a few other types). The Twelfth Air Force, based in North Africa, Sicily, and Italy, flew 430,681 sorties, losing 2,667 aircraft. Royal Air Force Bomber Command, though supposedly protected by flying at night, lost 55,573 men, a 20 percent casualty rate, greater than any single fighting force except the German U-boats. To be in a bomber of any kind during World War II was not a safe proposition.

Nevertheless, in spite of severe testing of even the highest morale, particularly during the summer and fall of 1943, American bomber crews did their jobs day after day, going up against the roughest flak and fighter defenses ever conceived. Because prewar planners believed bombers could get through without fighter protection had a great deal to do with the number of American losses. Army Air Forces commander General Henry H. "Hap" Arnold had the integrity to say it was the service's own fault that the P-51 did not arrive on the scene until late 1943.

When some bomber commanders remained stubbornly insistent that their bombers could still get through without fighters, Arnold quickly removed them from command, placed them elsewhere, and put aggressive believers in the fighter in their place. American bomber losses dropped from 9.1 percent per mission in October 1943 to 3.5 percent in March 1944 as long-range fighters engaged Luftwaffe fighters intent on getting to the bombers. By that time, planners had finally concentrated on what turned out to be the most vital enemy target, oil production, and the German war machine quickly ground to a halt in spite of increased industrial production.

Regardless of the continual banter between the bomber crews and the fighter pilots who flew escort for them, each held nothing but the highest respect for the other when it came down to doing their jobs. There was nothing more gut wrenching than watching a bomber go down out of control with men trapped inside . . . or a fighter outnumbered and trying to fight off a swarm of German fighters to protect the bombers, then getting clobbered in the process. There were no foxholes in the air.

As a companion volume to my book *Fighter Command* (Motorbooks International, 1991), *Bomber Command* has the same aim of turning a black-and-white war into one of color, brought to life with first person narrative. A few years ago I would have thought it nearly impossible to get enough vintage color to write more than one all-color book on World War II, but I have been proven wonderfully wrong by the generosity of the veterans and fellow historians who supplied the photos you see here. Fortunately for history, some Army Air Forces personnel carried their cameras, often against regulations, and asked for Kodachrome instead of cookies in their letters home.

To the following I owe a great debt of gratitude for trusting me to bring their wartime color to a new generation: Robert Astrella; Fred Bamberger; Duane J. Reed at the US Air Force Academy; Joe Kingsbury; Ole Griffith; Roger Freeman (for access to his files and for permission to quote interviews with Sam Wilson, John Ramsey, Lalli Coppinger, and Pecos Reeves); Arnold Delmonico; Byron Trent; Al Keeler (who also provided wartime memories); National Air & Space Museum staff members Dan Hagedorn, Melissa Keiser, Tim Cronen, and Mark Avino; Jack Havener (who provided not only his slides but also permission to quote from his excellent writing); Norman Jackson; Morris and Richard Davidson; Bill Skinner; James Wilson; Claude Porter; Lyle McCarty of the 459th Bomb Group Association (who also gave permission to quote from his wartime memoir *Coffee Tower*); John Devney, also of the 459th Bomb Group Association; David Menard; Mrs. M. M. Leigh; Jim Dietz; John Meyers; Albert Krassman; Roland Scott; Glenn Tessmer; Stan Piet; Leslie Peterson; Clark B. Rollins, Jr.; F. M. "Pappy" Grove (who also wrote an extensive series of recollections to go along with his slides); D. C. R. "Chris" Elliott and Andrew Renwick at the Royal Air Force Museum; Claude Murray and Ed Hoffman of the 7th Photo Group Association; Richard H. Denison; Jim Stitt; Herb Rutland; Cal Sloan; and Larry Hendel.

Photos alone could never bring the air war to life. The planes were maintained and flown by people who, happily, knew how to tell their experiences in such a way as to bring the reader back in time with them. That bomber war has come alive in a unique way thanks to all of you who took the time and effort to let me know how it really was: Bob DeGroat, both father and son (who provided an extensive series of memoirs called *Adventures in Military Flying* and *POW File*); Mark Hutchins (for interviews with Richard Fitzhugh, Bob Nourie, and Bud Abbot); Fred Alexander (for tapes of Corrine Wall and Bob Morgan); Ben Smith (for permission to quote from his book *Chick's Crew*, self-published, 1983); Tom Gabay (for sharing his father John's memoirs); Roy Kennett; Bob and Willetta Shoens; Bob Gillman (for permission to quote from his *Memoirs of War and Peace*); Mary Lou Neale; Charles Watry (for permission to quote from his book *Washout!*, California Aero Press, 1983); B. C. Reed; Philip Ardery (for permission to quote from his book *Bomber Pilot*, University Press of Kentucky, 1978); Ken Kailey; Ken Hamilton; Jim Bakewell; A. H. Albrecht; Ralph J. Watson, Jr. (for permission to quote from his father's memoirs); Fritz Nowosad; Hubert Cripe; Robert Keir; Ed Leighty; Johnny Miller; Frank Morrison; C. E. "Bud" Anderson (for permission to quote from his book *To Fly and Fight*, St. Martin's Press, 1990); Bud Guillot; Louis Kandl; George Meshko; Bob Kennedy; Alfred Price (my long time co-historian, who supplied a constant stream of material); Hans Iffland; Friedrich Stehle; Lowell Watts; John Flottorp; and Fred Weiner.

CHAPTER 1

Bomber Crew

Richard Fitzhugh
B-17 pilot, 457th Bomb Group

When I was a youngster, about five years old, my father was a traveling salesman. One week out of the month Ralph took him to one of the local country stores in the county. Sometimes he would take me with him. We stopped for lunch with sardines and the cheese box and crackers, and he would put me up on the counter when some of the lunch bunch at the country store would come by, and he'd say, "Dickie, what do you want to be when you grow up?" I'd say, "I want to fight the Germans!" I don't know where I got this from. This would be in about 1927. I was born in 1922. I guess somewhere in my early youth I'd been hearing about World War I, but this was in my mind. I started early in making model airplanes of balsa wood. I'd take them up on the roof of the house, line them up, set them on fire, and watch them go sailing off.

Of course, I knew about Lindbergh. I remember a barnstormer came to our hometown of Charlottesville, Virginia. I must have been probably seven years old at this point, and I wanted to go touch the airplane. The sign said, "Don't touch." I wanted to go touch it anyway, and the pilot came over, and very gruffly said, "Get away! You might stick your finger through it." I was taken aback a little bit.

Somehow or other I had just developed an interest in airplanes. I used to go up to Washington, D.C., and spend summers out on Columbia Pike in Arlington. At that time, the national airport was Hoover Field, where the Pentagon is now. They had a swimming pool there—the airport swimming pool. We would walk down Columbia Pike to the swimming pool; you could walk across the runway in those days. They had a gate like you do at a railroad track. We'd go down there and watch what was known then as the "Great Silver Fleet" take off: beautiful Eastern Airlines and American Airlines airplanes. I think it was Eastern that was called the "Great Silver Fleet." These were all C-47s and DC-3s. Just spectacular as a kid to stand there by the run-

Bomber transition B-17Fs at sunset after a long day surviving the rigors of teaching new crews how to handle a heavy bomber. Zone of Interior (ZI or stateside) training aircraft were worn out at a furious pace, from both use and accidents. Never before had such a large-scale experiment been attempted in teaching neophytes to handle state-of-the-art technology. *USAF*

The Air Corps that was, and was never to be again, in the calm before the storm. These US Army Air Corps officers and their beautiful friends stand in front of the massive Boeing XB-15 at Bolling Field, Washington, D.C., in the winter snow of 1940. Though the underpowered B-15 was never destined to be much more than a prototype, it paved the way for heavy bomber development, the core of airpower doctrine that would shape the strategies of World War II. *NASM Arnold Collection*

way and watch these things go. I think some of that had to do with me wanting to get into the Army Air Corps. I wasn't much into the movies; I'd much rather be making model airplanes and setting them on fire or watching the real thing!

One day I was out to lunch, and I passed the recruiting station. Big signs out there showed the B-17—all these beautiful recruiting posters. Somebody was with me, and we both decided to go in and sign up, so we did. Just like that. That was in May of '42, and they didn't call me until October.

B. C. Reed
B-18 copilot, 17th Bomb Group

This little boy's dream came true when I graduated from the Air Corps Advanced Fly-ing School, Class of 40-E, at Kelly Field, Texas, on August 30, 1940, as a second lieutenant, US Army Air Corps, with rating as pilot. "I wanted Wings." Now I officially wore silver wings! And a Sam Browne belt with a saber. Wow!

Several of us became copilots in the three squadrons of the 17th Group. We didn't realize it at the time, but we were enjoying the last days of the old peacetime Air Corps, with Wednesday and Friday afternoons off, and completely free weekends (one Saturday morning a month we had a dress parade). We were considered "student officers" for three more months, with more ground school.

We expected to remain copilots and second lieutenants for years. In 1940, second

lieutenants were told to expect serving seven years before making first lieutenant, and then *at least* five more years before even being considered for captain, *if* we were good enough to still be on active duty.

Bob DeGroat
PT-23 pilot, primary flight training

At one point we got alternating aerobatic maneuvers. I could hardly wait to get in my snap-and-a-half specialty. I announced my intentions and concentrated hard. The maneuver came out solidly and precisely. As I proudly looked into the rearview mirror for approval and respect from my instructor in the rear cockpit, I was horrified to see nobody there. I immediately righted the trainer and began sweeping turns, looking for a parachute or a falling body. At last I saw a slight bobbing motion in the rear cockpit and recognized the top of a helmet just barely showing as it rocked with mirth.

My instructor had lowered his seat to the bottom while I was preparing my show-off maneuver and curled himself out of sight. He finished me off with his own top maneuver, which was to go inverted, do two clearing turns while inverted, and then enter into an inverted spin.

I knew when I'd been topped.

A brand spanking new Boeing B-17D Flying Fortress assigned to Wright Field's Air Development Center for service tests in 1941. Advanced versions of this single type would dominate wartime planning, carrying a new generation of crews into combat around the world. In spite of prewar isolationism, the "Fort" was ready for mass production on a hitherto unheard of scale. *NASM Groenhoff Collection*

13

Engine change on an early Douglas A-20 Havoc during the 1941 Louisiana Maneuvers, which attempted for the first time to combine air and ground forces in some form of cohesive whole. Lighter attack aircraft (most twin-engine types) were the other side of the newly renamed US Army Air Forces' bomber doctrine. There was some serious attention to tactical, or close air support, aviation, though this aspect of the service was somewhat of a stepchild. That would change drastically by 1944, when tactical air forces were looked upon as vital to moving troops forward in the field. *NASM Arnold Collection*

Charles Watry
PT-22 pilot, primary flight training

Dubbed the "Maytag Messerschmitt," the PT-22 had a fighter-plane look about it and handled as well as a fighter, too. The engine had a distinctive *pockata-pockata* sound to it, giving the impression of a slow-turning engine, which it was. Even on takeoff, the engine sounded as if it were not turning up enough revs to get the trainer off the ground.

Ben Smith
B-17 radio operator, 303rd Bomb Group

We came east on a troop train that seemed to make no progress at all. It toiled on for days, chugging and wheezing and clanking along, stopping for hours at a time, then backing up for miles, then stopping and starting again. Our route took us through the Royal Gorge of Colorado, the only bright spot of the trip. Sometimes we would sit on a siding, sweating and dirty, as a streamliner flashed by us at lightning speed, compounding our discomfort. We could see the fat cats in the dining car giving us the fish eye over their horn-rimmed spectacles as they had their morning coffee, ham and eggs, and newspapers. We ate our powdered eggs and cursed them roundly. The troop trains were pulled by the old iron-horse locomotives. Because of the heat we rode with

Shortly after the attack on Pearl Harbor, many Army and Navy units were assigned to coastal patrol because of fear of an enemy invasion. One of the more promising new medium bombers in line squadrons at the time was the North American B-25 Mitchell. This B-25A of the 2nd Bomb Group was based on the East Coast in early 1942 for antisubmarine patrol. *NASM Arnold Collection*

15

With the B-17E, which first rolled out in September 1941, came the definitive shape of the Flying Fortress that would become so famous in World War II. With numerous improvements, particularly in defensive fire power, and with the addition of a tail gunner's position, this version carried the brunt of the Army Air Forces' initial strategic bombing effort over Europe and the Pacific. *USAF*

the windows up. There was no air conditioning. The cinders were flying about like sooty snowflakes. Rivulets of dirty sweat streamed down our faces, our clothes became filthy, and we stank abominably. Of all the humbling experiences I ever had, there was nothing to compare with a troop train.

Right off the bat O'Hearn and I got caught for being out of uniform and were put on K.P. for the duration of the trip eastward. It was not so great a transgression—they needed some full time K.P.s, and we were elected. One of the cars was set aside for the preparation and cooking of food. We had been on duty for eighteen hours and

were about to go off. I had a bright idea. We would make some bologna sandwiches, wrap them up in wax paper, and peddle them to the officers. This was no problem as we had the kitchen to ourselves. We did a land-office business for the rest of the trip and made a lot of money. The mess officer could not understand what was happening to all his bologna. We did not enlighten him.

Ken Hamilton
AT-6 mechanic, factory airfield

At times us Yanks got a good dose of British upper-class ways, and it wasn't often we could get some satisfaction. Few of us

A never-to-be-forgotten sight for a new Army Air Forces cadet: the entrance to the West Point of the air, Randolph Field, Texas, where the Army centered the training of its pilots. When President Franklin Roosevelt issued his prewar call for building 50,000 planes a year, the military services pushed up their student pilot quotas to meet the demand. This influx of men and machines proved to be a crucial factor in helping the United States to withstand the early dark days of World War II. *Fred E. Bamberger*

will forget one of the arrivals made by the British squadron leader assigned to American factories in southern California. Approaching from the east in a Douglas Boston, he started to let down with the gear up. The North American and Douglas flight ramp mechanics ran out, wildly waving, trying to get him to go around. He looked out the open left side of the cockpit window, acknowledged the waving with a snappy salute, flared beautifully at gear-down height, plopped onto the runway, and slid to a halt. He climbed out, strode rapidly to a car, and left without a word.

Bob DeGroat
BT-13 pilot, basic flight training

Stages could be considered as landing performance exams. They taxied a BT over to the west side of the field and used it as a radio control and reviewing stand for the instructors who were to do the evaluating. The cadets were to make four three-point landings. Evaluation was based on approach, landing control, form, and proximity to a hypothetical spot directly in front of the parked control plane.

As luck would have it, I was really "on" this day. I strung together probably the best four BT landings that I ever made, and stuck them in with my wing tip dead in front of the "judges." After my fourth landing (which I thought at the time was only ordinary), I got a faint, garbled instruction that disappointingly did not release me to return to the main field, but to make still another landing. So I took off again and came around for landing—only this time I overshot a little.

To set it down right in front of the con-

trol plane, I had to fly it onto the ground with the tail high. I had no sooner done this when the radio exploded again in unintelligible chaos, ending with sending me back to the main field.

The mystery was cleared up when I next saw my instructor. He greeted me with, "Boy, did you put on a show yesterday! You not only put in four perfect landings, but when they asked you to try an extra one and make it a wheel landing, you stuck that one in, too." I never let on.

Ben Smith
B-17 radio operator, 303rd Bomb Group

The B-17 was never used as a night bomber, yet strangely enough, almost all of our cross-country flying training was done at night. Once on a night mission we were almost involved in a midair collision, the first of many. There were no radar stations handling air traffic, as nowadays. Our mission took us by Pensacola, Florida, where there was a big naval flying school. We blundered right into the traffic pattern of a bunch of student pilots shooting night landings. Chick pulled sharply to miss one airplane that was heading straight toward us. We had it hot and heavy there for a few moments. All of us went to the windows to watch out for the tiny airplanes that were buzzing all around us. I'll bet we scared them a lot worse than they scared us.

Bob DeGroat
AT-10 pilot, advanced twin engine flight training

The last day before graduation (which

The "Washing Machine" . . . there was no better description of the Boeing Stearman PT-17 Kaydet. For most cadets, this was the first aircraft they would fly in primary—a rude awakening for most. Large and prone to ground-looping because of its narrow landing gear and a high center of gravity, this aircraft was very difficult for inexperienced pilots to master, getting its nickname from "washing out" so many cadets from flight training. *NASM Groenhoff Collection*

meant receiving your wings and lieutenant's bars at last) was supposed to be a relaxed, fun flying day. The assignment was a low-level cross-country designed to sharpen identification of physical checkpoints and map reading, but was understood by student and instructor alike to be a legalized "buzz job." In my own case, during the early moments of the trip, every time I glanced at my instructor in the copilot seat, his hand seemed to subtly indicate that I was too high. It was great fun. We went down val-leys, climbed over tree lines and high ten-sion wires, scared some livestock, and even startled a few people driving on the high-way.

Bob Gillman
B-24 pilot, advanced four engine bomber transition

Following graduation, my orders were to go to the Student Training Detachment at Smyrna, Tennessee, which was twelve miles south of Nashville, for transition into the B-

Eric W. Holtz with a Stearman during primary at Union City, Tennessee, in the summer of 1943. Clearly the airplane has been worked hard—with fading, old Army Air Corps blue and yellow paint, nonstandard by this time, and a replacement aileron painted with silver dope. No one was really worried about matching paint because of the hectic pace of training so many pilots. *Albert J. Keeler*

The view from Army cadet Ole Griffith's primary training PT-17 at Dorr Field, Alabama, in 1943. The flight line was always crowded and always busy, with instructors, students, and linemen sending a continual stream of junior birdmen into the air. Though the Stearman was a throwback to an earlier age of baling wire and fabric biplanes, it was an excellent introduction to handling large aircraft prone to ground loops. *Ole C. Griffith*

24 Liberator bomber. SAAF [Smyrna Army Air Field] was an excellent base with mostly brick buildings, an officers club, and bachelor officer quarters. Other facilities included an officers bowling alley, swimming pools, and several Hamburger Havens, even on the flight line. Now, this was a "real" military air base, where flying took place around the clock. Nevertheless, we were still basking in the glory of being saluted and addressed as "Sir!" We also realized that this was where the really serious business began.

On February 25, 1944, we were taken down to the flight line and shown the B-24. Four student officers were assigned to an instructor, who spent two hours going over the entire aircraft, inside and out. I will never

forget climbing up on the flight deck and seeing the cockpit for the first time. The instrument panel stretched from the extreme left to the extreme right of the cockpit and was covered entirely with instruments. There were controls and levers on the left side of the pilot's area from the front panel to behind the seat back, and from the window sill to the floor. Same on the right side. The center pedestal held not only the four throttles, but also four mixture controls, four turbocharger controls, four propeller controls, four cowl flap switches, and four of many other things. Landing gear and flap levers were by the pilot's and copilot's knees, respectively. Even the ceiling was covered with radio controls from front to rear and left to right. Immediately below the landing

The intermediate training step in an Army pilot's career was basic, where the Vultee BT-13 Valiant provided a bit more complexity. Better known as the "Virbrator," this fixed gear, 450 horsepower craft had most of the systems common to more advanced types, including a controllable-pitch propeller and flaps. For the most part, pilots couldn't wait to get out of basic flight training and into their advanced phase. *Fred E. Bamberger*

gear lever, by the pilot's right leg, was a red "T" handle, which was the bomb salvo lever. Pulled up to the first notch, it opened the bomb bay doors. Pulling further to the limit dropped the entire bomb load. This was obviously a true emergency control, which I did not realize at that moment would be used before the year 1944 was past. Needless to say, we were all overwhelmed by what we had just witnessed and hardly believed we would ever master this cockpit!

Bob DeGroat
B-24 pilot, advanced four engine bomber transition

My first close-up examination of a Con-

solidated B-24 Liberator was to stand up and view the inside through the lower waist hatch of a parked aircraft. I looked in wonder at the barn-like space, having only just graduated from Globe AT-10s. I had been quoted in my early transition training as comparing the flight deck visibility in the B-24 to "flying a hotel from the basement window."

Visualize a flight line full of fledgling pilots all trying to taxi their first tricycle-geared aircraft. It not only has twice the engines and throttles, but also is twice the size of anything they have handled before. Note that this is under the impatient guidance of disgruntled instructors who are trying to get off the ground and on with their boring day of instructing extremely green pilots.

One of the first instructions that my co-student received when he first got in the left seat was to adjust the seat fore-and-aft and up-and-down to get comfortable, then check his position so he could be assured of making the same seat adjustments the next time. Therefore, when it became time for me to take the left seat in the air midway through the flying period, I looked for a surefire check for seat height. Looking out the window on my side, I found that I could just see the marker light on the wing tip over the outboard engine nacelle.

The next day, when it was my turn to be first in the left seat, I tried to use this check

Intrepid Army basic student Ole Griffith climbs into his BT-13 at Gunter Field, Alabama, September 1943 on his way to becoming a photo-mapping pilot in F-10s, the photo version of the B-25 Mitchell. *Ole C. Griffith*

Lieutenant Johnny King flying a North American BT-14 out of Randolph Field, Texas, May 1942. Though the BT-14 looked a great deal like its bigger brother, the AT-6, it was actually an older fixed gear aircraft with less power and a fabric-covered fuselage. When the BT-13 became available in large numbers, the older '14 left the scene, having served since well before the beginning of the war. *Fred E. Bamberger*

23

At last—advanced twin-engine pilot training. A Beechcraft AT-10 Wichita from Freeman Field, Indiana, late 1943. The AT-10 was a wood-and-fabric airplane with a single purpose for existence: getting multi-engine pilots trained as fast as possible and pushing them into operational units. As a result, the AT-10 was born, lived, and died all within the war years. *Ole C. Griffith*

to adjust the seat height, but my head hit the canopy and my feet wouldn't reach the rudder pedals. That long Davis wing of the B-24 was very limber and flexed as much as three feet in flight—I had proof. Later, on a cross-country trip in turbulent air, I was able to see motion not unlike a jump rope when I viewed the wing from the nose compartment. Impressive, but quite frightening.

I was familiar with engine-out procedures, with their accompanying drag and corrective trim techniques, from flying the Globe AT-10 in Advanced Training. However, I was not ready for the drag problems of an outboard engine failure in the B-24. For-

tunately, the rudder pedals on the B-24 were large enough to accommodate both feet, and I was encouraged to do this by my instructor, at least until I became familiar enough with the engine-out procedure to get corrective trim in quickly. Some instructors, mine included, might occasionally "pull" an outboard engine on you and then refuse to let you use trim for correction. The alternative was to put both feet on the one pedal to hold opposite rudder, lock your knees, then hope that your seat belt was snug enough to keep you from sliding up the back of the seat. It didn't take long for the strain to set your legs to quaking from the unrelieved pres-

The Cessna AT-17, or UC-78, Bobcat served across the United States as a multi-engine advanced trainer. Originally developed as a civil light transport, Cessna's first twin came along at just the right time to be ordered in great numbers for the war effort. Nicknamed the "Bamboo Bomber" for its wood-and-fabric construction, the bulbous aircraft got stuck with a number of other less flattering names, including the "Useless 78" and the "Double-Breasted Cub." *USAF*

Another in a string of advanced multi-trainers was the Curtiss AT-9 Jeep, certainly the oddest and the most difficult twin to handle of the lot. With only two seats, the jeep was small, a beast of a ground-looper, and difficult to fly on one engine. If a pilot got through its quirks and graduated, he could fly just about anything given to him. *USAF*

sure. Many a sadistic instructor took out his frustrations in viewing the vibrating, sweating student that he had created.

Bob Nourie
B-26 pilot, advanced twin engine bomber transition

We flew a few copilot missions in AT-23s or the B-26, towing targets in planes that were being flown by the WASP pilots—some of the most experienced WASP pilots that they had. Boy, those girls could fly. They were people with a lot of flying time, cer-

tainly more experienced than most new military pilots. These were relatively young women. Those very experienced ones were in their thirties, maybe thirty-five, thirty-eight. Very experienced pilots. I flew copilot for some of those. Some of them flew B-24s, and they had to practice for the gunners.

Mary Lou Neale
A-20 pilot, Women Airforce Service Pilot

In ferrying, love of flying *had* to win over fondness for comfort, if one wanted to stay in that command. Primary trainers and fight-

When bombardiers went to school, they flew in the Beechcraft AT-11 fitted with a Norden bombsight, a full set of bomb release gadgets, and an internal bomb bay—just like the real thing. These AT-11s are heading back from the range to the SAAAF Bomb School at Concho, Texas, January 1943 with their cadet bombardiers aboard. *Fred E. Bamberger*

A bombardier cadet (left) sits with his instructor in the nose of a SAAAF Bomb School AT-11, January 1943. Quite often these men were washed-out, would-be pilots assigned to bombardier or navigator school, much to their disappointment. The stigma was one not easily gotten over, though bombardiers were crucial to the success of the bombers' missions. At least pilots had a skill they could transfer to peacetime. What would a bombardier do? *Fred E. Bamberger*

27

An AT-11 is fueled up on the line at Ontario Army Air Base, California, in late 1944. The snow-capped mountains to the north formed a stunning backdrop to this field, which primarily served as a major P-38 transition base. The AT-11s had to fly over this range to get to the dry lake bed bombing range at Muroc, an ideal site for dropping all kinds of exploding ordnance.
Norman W. Jackson

ers had one thing in common—both had miserable cockpits for the long haul. One was either hot or cold, rattling around in a windswept cavern or cramped into a miniature oven. But now and then appeared a miracle—like the cushiony A-20. Orders to take this sturdy beauty with its luxurious armchair in a glassed-in room to Canada seemed like a gift too good to be true. It was. There was another name on it: "Staff Sergeant Louis Stamp, Radio Operator." These A-20s, named "Bostons" by the British, were not equipped with cockpit radio for ferrying, so a crew member sitting in the nose was necessary.

Staff Sergeant Stamp turned out to be a short, muscular, stone-faced veteran of few words, mostly grunts. On rotation after overseas duty, he and four other sergeants were to operate the radio for the five A-20s destined for Montreal. The other four pilots were male. It was obvious that none of the noncoms had ever *seen* a woman fly a military plane. From the sudden silence when I appeared and the grim set of his jaw, it was also obvious that disciplined Stamp had been taking a bit of ribbing. It presaged to be one long, disagreeable flight from my Palm Springs base.

Luck and some corrective measures came into play. First, my plane was ready to go, so we took off immediately, leaving the skeptics behind. Then it was time for some hedge-hopping (no witnesses a necessity) to illustrate pilot aptitude. Somewhere over the southern tip of the Sierra Nevadas, the doughty sergeant broke. "Lady, I'm convinced. You can fly. If you'll get a little altitude, I can tune in some music for you, okay?" So I relaxed while he, presumably mollified, guided us towards Albuquerque. Once on the ground, another surprise awaited him. *Girls* (WACS) were refueling the planes. They waved companionably to me and flirted gently with him. All parties were delighted. And the A-20 could not have been

A newly graduated bombardier gets his wings from his sweetheart, along with a gleaming new pair of second lieutenant's "brown" bars. Before long, the hat will have its stiffener removed so it can be crumpled and mashed into a "fifty-mission crush." Moments like this made the Army Air Forces live up to its reputation as the "glamour boy" service. But that image wouldn't count for much in a few months, when the fly boys would be under attack from intense flak and determined enemy fighters. *USAF*

Upon getting one's wings, whether as a pilot, bombardier, navigator, radioman, flight engineer, or gunner, the next stop was bomber transition at a stateside training base devoted to a specific type of aircraft. This B-17F, with standard four-digit white training numbers on the tail, heads out on a practice mission. *Albert J. Keeler*

After graduating from twin-engine advanced, Jack Havener took his first operational training unit ride in this B-26 Marauder at Drane Field, Lakeland, Florida, in October 1943. Known as the "Widow Maker" due to so many accidents, the Marauder had a higher landing speed than most bombers, demanding the utmost attention to the airspeed indicator on final approach. By the end of the war, the '26 was rated as one of the Army Air Forces' most effective aircraft. *Jack K. Havener*

30

in better hands. So I set the time for the next morning and got a ride into town. It was obvious that my "crew" needed no further assistance.

Proof indeed was the WAC send-off in the early dawn: "Bye, Louie! See ya again!" Then, since it was Saturday morning, I listened to the opera and Stamp listened to his baseball game, in between his radio reporting. We were flying "over the top." The world was beautiful and unreal, only miles of white cotton beneath the A-20 and Verdi in the ears. Then came a request. The weather sounded not too great for our destination. How about putting into "St. Joe" to check it out? Sounded like good advice, so we did. The weather did close in, and, surprise of

surprises, Staff Sergeant Stamp had a sick aunt in St. Joseph, so we RON'ed [remained overnight] in conscience. I arranged a ride into town for myself, since the sergeant assured me that his cousin would drive out for him. When I arrived at the airport the next morning, he was already there—asleep on a bench. He had to stay up all night with his sick aunt, the poor man.

We were now a real team, the best of pals, sharing a mutual admiration. I had to give him an "A" for apparent stamina—which needed no words. In fact, the only words I recall him saying to me, which were not directly related to navigation or radio, was a phrase used as the highest compliment in those long-ago days: "You ought to

Stateside practice mission. An early model B-25 is loaded with practice bombs for a trip to the range. Though trainee crews—particularly those in the hot Southwest—thought such flying would never end, the common complaint was not enough training by the time they got to the combat theaters. That the Army Air Forces produced the first-rate bomber crews it did is a credit to that service's "can do" attitude, from General Hap Arnold on down. *USAF*

be in the movies!" We returned from Montreal by different routes, and by the time I had delivered a P-39 and was back at Palm Springs again, he had been transferred. But there was a box of candy in my BOQ with the note, "Lady, I would fly with you again anytime. You're a good pilot. I told those guys too. Sincerely, Louis F. Stamp, Jr. Staff Sergeant"

Bob Gillman
B-24 pilot, advanced four engine bomber transition

We flew just about every day and some nights and started doing a lot of formation flying. We were getting to know each other individually and began melting together as a crew. Naturally, we had no doubts that our crew was the best! I got a kick when Ed Caley, our top turret gunner and assistant engineer, told me that some of our guys had made bets with some men on another crew that we could fly a closer formation than them on today's scheduled formation flight. After takeoff, we formed up on the right wing of the lead ship (number two position), while they were on the left wing.

Now, as it happened, I loved to fly formation and worked very hard learning to fly tight and smooth. You must learn to almost

A fledgling F-10 Mitchell crew heads out over the Colorado flatlands from Peterson Field on a practice photo mission. The trimetrigon camera equipped B-25 was an ideal mapping platform—stable, long-ranged, and easy to fly. *Ole C. Griffith*

Being a Women Airforce Service Pilot (WASP) was every bit as thrilling as these WASPs in front of a Lockheed Lodestar at the Army Air Forces Fighter Gunnery School, Foster Field, Victoria, Texas, late 1944 seem to think it is. When the WASPs were phased out in December 1944, most offered to stay on for nothing as long as they could fly the fighters, bombers, and transports they had come to love. From left to right are Pauline S. Cutler, Dorothy Erhardt, Jennie M. Hill, Etta Mae Hollinger, Lucille R. Cary, Jane B. Shirley, Dorothy H. Beard, and Kathryn L. Boyd. Their jobs included ferrying aircraft, towing targets, and instrument instruction. Of the 1,104 women who became WASPs, forty-one were killed in the line of duty. *USAF*

A veteran bomber transition B-17D was pulled off the line to star as *Mary Ann* in one of the better wartime films on the Army Air Forces—*Air Force*, starring John Garfield. The film followed the fortunes of a single Fort from its flying into the attack on Pearl Harbor to the invasion of Wake Island. *Mary Ann* is seen here after the filming, back at her training field, on 6 April 1943. *USAF*

anticipate the need to add or reduce power *before* you actually begin to slide slowly back or forward, and I was getting this down to a science. Tom would watch my every move closely and would get so frustrated when he could see my hand moving the throttles for-ward ever so slightly and wondered why, because he could not see that we were falling back. Rather, we did not move at all, or, I could sense that we were about to drop back and would add a little power and, again, we didn't move at all.

As crews headed overseas, they often took mascots with them, though that was strictly against Army regulations. There had to be very few cats in the world that could live with the in-flight noise of a B-25, but pilot Ole Griffith proved the point by snapping the 90th Photo Mapping Squadron cat in flight over Peru in 1944. *Ole C. Griffith*

It was very smooth today, and I kept inching closer and closer, "sticking the wing tip in the waist window," as it used to be called, until I was satisfied, then held it right there, even during turns. Actually, close formation flying is really dangerous, especially among low time pilots in 65,000-pound large airplanes. Once a heavy aircraft starts moving, especially in the wrong direction, you have no way of "putting on the brakes" to stop the movement. Midair collisions were not uncommon, especially in combat, where every aircraft took off well over gross weight and was very hard to handle in formation. After we landed, our guys were smiling and told us the next day that they made a few bucks.

Corrine Wall
widow of B-24 copilot Jack Wall, 392nd Bomb Group

Words can never express the feelings families have when their young men are sent out to kill or be killed—no matter how noble the cause may seem to be—for there is no winner as the cream of that generation dies. Only by living through this period can anyone really feel the pains of war.

A son missing for a year, constant hope that he'll be found. Asking for help from the Red Cross to find information and then having their reply blocked just prior to reaching you. Needing your other son to hold as you grieve for the lost one, but not being able to do so. Knowing your son would never have been flying and would possibly still be alive had you never signed parental permission papers. Replacing the little flag in the window that had two blue stars (two sons in the service) with two flags—one with a blue star and one with a gold star (one killed).

A baby who would never know her father. A body returned six years after death with only officials stating he was your son. Many years of movies being made that glorified war and not being able to watch them because the pain was still so real. These things are so private, and yet we who remember *must* convey them to our sons and daughters, for only through God can we have life, and that abundantly!

John Gabay
B-24 tail gunner, advanced bomber transition

When I completed armament school at Salt Lake City, I was shipped to Tucson, Arizona, to join a B-24 Liberator training group. I would have preferred B-17s, but it didn't matter too much as long as I got on a crew

One of the major jumping off points for the European Theater of Operations was Goose Bay, Labrador, where the base ground crew is giving this B-25 the standard treatment for snow and ice prevention: Cover the whole thing with tarps, let it snow or sleet like mad, then pull off the tarps. It sure beat having the aircraft stranded and out of action for an indefinite period of time. *Morris Davidson via Richard Davidson*

and started flying. I was anxious to find out what kind of crew I was assigned to, and it wasn't long before I found out. We met under the wing of the ship. I was the tail gunner and armorer. Then we met our officers: Lieutenant Huie, the pilot, from Ark-ansas; Lieutenant Kemp, our bombardier, from Chicago; Lieutenant Glickman, our navigator, also from Chicago. No copilot was assigned to us. The reason was that our pilot was such a poor flyer that we always had an instructor for a copilot. Our navigator was another beauty. He couldn't find the field one day and took us into Mexico. But our bombardier took the cake. We were supposed to be on a night practice bombing mission over the desert. Instead, he dropped a 100-pound smoke bomb through the roof of a house in the suburbs of Tucson. Our enlisted men

had the highest marks in the group; our officers were the lowest.

Roy Kennett
B-24 radio operator, advanced bomber transition

You know, I didn't even want to be a radio operator. I wanted to be a gunner, and I was a *good* gunner. Little did I know the only one on a B-24 who doesn't have a gun is the radio operator. I went to school at Fort Myers and got a top-notch shooting record, but they told me "You've got to have another technical school. You can't be just a gunner. You need something in conjunction with that." I'd heard that Armorer's School was in a mudhole down in Biloxi, Mississippi, and the engineers went to some God-awful place near Brownsville, Texas. Now radio school

was in St. Louis, Illinois. So I said, "Yep! Send me to radio school. I'm going to *Saint Looey*!" I went to St. Louis just because it was the best place to go. They turned me into a gunner without a gun.

Bob Gillman, B-24 pilot, bomber debarkation pool

We spent three days at Grenier and were issued many additional items. We took off from Grenier on July 25, 1944, at 1500 and landed at Presque Isle, Army Air Base, Maine, at 1700 for additional equipment. We were certain that this would surely be our last stop in the USA, and we all felt it would be only proper that we should go into town and do a little partying. We were assigned quarters, but for some reason we were told to leave our baggage in the airplane. We all

went down to the line, got dressed, and proceeded to the main gate to see if we could get transportation to Presque Isle. However, we were stopped short by the guard, who advised us that only officers were allowed off the base; enlisted men were restricted to the base. We argued vehemently with the guard, to no avail. He had his orders. We all stepped outside then, quite upset that we could not be together as a crew to have some fun on our last night in the States.

Then one of my officers, who shall remain nameless, suggested a very simple plan that would solve this problem. We all walked down to the flight line to the airplane and dug into our baggage again. Twenty minutes later, ten officers walked back to the main gate. We never really knew if that guard recognized any of our faces. However, after proper salutes were ex-

A line of new B-17Es at Goose Bay, staging for the European Theater of Operations, 1942. These early Fortresses were the mainstay of the Eighth Air Force's early penetrations at Nazi-occupied Europe, testing German defenses as well as their abilities at daylight precision bombing, an unproven doctrine. In the years to come, thousands of men would fight and die to make precision bombing a key cog in the Allied plan to defeat Hitler. *Morris Davidson via Richard Davidson*

changed, we all caught a bus and headed to town. I took time to explain to our enlisted men what a serious offense it was to impersonate an officer, but no one seemed overly concerned. In fact, they were already enjoying returning salutes. I also told them that if anyone got into trouble and was not back in the morning, he would be left behind if we had to leave. We then separated and proceeded to have a great time. Sure, it was a stupid thing to do, but someone must have been watching over us that night, and it really brought us closer together as a crew.

Willetta Shoens
wife of B-17 pilot Bob Shoens, 100th Bomb Group

I sat at home next to the radio, devouring the newspaper, adding to the wartime scrapbook I was assembling to keep track of the missions Bob was flying. As a young wife, waiting at home, you just naturally assumed that your husband went on every raid. On March the 4, we learned that our best man had died in the first raid on Berlin. You just pray that *your* man is going to come home. You can't help but be selfish about it.

37

CHAPTER 2

Mediterranean Theater of Operations

Bob DeGroat
B-24 pilot, 459th Bomb Group

My first flight in Italy was an adventure in itself. The first pilot and pseudo-tour director (I flew the right seat) was a veteran flier who had completed his tour and was waiting for transportation back to the States. The plane was a war-weary B-24 that had six-by-six boards in the bottom of the bomb bay and was used as a freight carrier.

The idea was to load my "green" crew aboard and show them the local area and its landmarks, so we wouldn't get lost when we were on our own. The flight was pleasant: We checked out the gold dome of the cathedral at Cerignola, took a look at the lighthouse and cliffs that make up the spur of the boot as seen on any map of Italy, and buzzed some fishing boats. All went well until we returned to make a landing.

This was an early model of the B-24 that had a warning horn that sounded if you retarded the throttles without having the landing gear locked down. There were also light indicators for the gear position. In our first attempt at lowering the gear, the horn was silent, but the indicators showed that one of the main gears was not locked. We recycled the landing gear, and this time the indicators were satisfactory, but the warning horn went off. We recycled over and over, but something always refused to check out.

We finally threw out the nose gear manually and cranked the main gear down by hand, trying to get everything locked in place properly. At last the yellow-painted main gear latches looked from the waist section to be correct. All the indicators were green, and the warning horn remained silent. I double-checked everything on the base leg, and things were fine. We turned on final, and shortly thereafter the warning horn sounded briefly, but went silent again.

We touched down gently and began to slow when the warning horn came on again as the right main gear started to retract. Suddenly the gear snapped back into place and the horn was quiet once more. The plane had slowed to what I estimate to be

The mainstay of Army Air Forces bomber operations in North Africa was the B-25 Mitchell, which was able to take the rough and tumble operations of flying through sandstorm takeoffs and harsh conditions. A B-25C attached to the 321st Bomb Group, *Oh-7*, and crew prepare to take off on a mission from their Tunisian base. *USAF*

In January 1944, when the 344th Bomb Group left as a unit with their B-26s for England on the South Atlantic Ferry Route, they had no idea they'd be stuck for almost a month in Marrakech, Morocco. After getting all the Marauders to Africa in February, the weather closed in, preventing them from making the final leg to England. What else to do but see the sites? This local bus was the most modern form of transportation available. *Jack K. Havener*

sixty to seventy miles per hour, when the horn again came on, and the left main gear retracted completely into the wing. The left wing tip hit the ground, causing the wing to crack at the root and drag to the rear at an odd angle. The nose gear broke off. The upper turret came off its track and swung by its guns between the pilot and me.

I flipped the switches off and unbuckled to get out. The engineer had gone out the top hatch like a rocket, run down the wing, and was a quarter mile away. There was all kinds of dust in the air, but I couldn't detect any smoke, fumes, or fire (but I wasn't far behind the engineer). They towed the wreckage to the bone yard, and I never heard anything but thanks for getting rid of that lemon.

That's not where the story ended. One, the officers of each crew had a tent in the olive orchard up on the hill that they called home. It was late fall and our newly erected tent had no heater. The holdup was the lack of a hard-to-find petcock to control the flow of captured German gasoline into our rudimentary stove. After our crash landing, the dust had not yet settled before my bombardier was back in the plane trying to pry a petcock out with his bare hands.

Then I made my next landing in Italy. To this point, I had never made a normal landing on a gravel runway. The first landing, as indicated above, was a noisy affair, so you can imagine my first thoughts when loose gravel was kicked up against the bottom of the fuselage as I let the nose wheel down in

After the first B-17s had arrived in North Africa, combat damage quickly took its toll, a preview of things to come. Quickly stripped of useful items to keep others flying, this 97th Bomb Group hulk was put to good use as a training aid for ditching, an ever-present possibility regardless of theater of operation. These 414th Squadron crewmen were a part of the unit's move up through Algeria and Tunisia in 1942 and 1943. *USAF*

Mt. Vesuvius rumbles in the distance beyond this 47th Bomb Group A-20 Havoc and some 31st Fighter Group Spitfire Vs at Pomigliano, Italy, in late 1943. When the volcano finally erupted in 1944, it virtually destroyed the 340th Bomb Group's B-25s, something the Luftwaffe was never able to pull off. *William J. Skinner*

a normal landing. My hair stood on end for a second, as I thought I had another collapsed gear.

Philip Ardery
B-24 squadron commander, 389th Bomb Group

Before I started combat, the most important question in my mind was how I would take it. I knew I had no more courage than the average American, but I had studiously followed the methods suggested by psychologists to overcome fear. Early in my flying career I discovered that when you have an airplane in your hands and you feel yourself getting scared, the first thing you must do is force yourself to relax. If you become tense, you completely lose that all-important feel of the controls that gives advance warning of what the ship is likely to do. You know what kind of glide to set for landing. You know whether you have enough speed to clear the tree ahead of you, or you know if you try to clear it, you will stall out at a critically low altitude. Then you must plan to point the nose of your ship down and let the tree take a wing off to break the forward motion as the plane pancakes it. I have prayed

Red Cross girl Helen Ellor serving coffee and doughnuts to a tired bunch of 320th Bomb Group Marauder crews on Corsica after a mission in 1944. There was nothing quite so beautiful as the sight of these wonderful gals, always ready with a smile and some conversation. That such lambs survived in a den of wolves was a tribute to their stamina and dedication. *Joseph S. Kingsbury*

for a greater capacity to keep cool in pinches, because I know that panic may be the equivalent of suicide. If I maintain calm, I think there is a good chance I can land an airplane in any sort of terrain without injuring myself.

My first few missions hit me just about the way I thought they would. Sometimes I was scared, but on the easier runs I didn't feel much more than a pleasant exhilaration. Still, when the flak started breaking right against my airplane, or when I saw the enemy fighters practically flying through our waist windows, I could feel my pulse rise. Particularly, if I saw one of our ships filled with friends of mine sprout flames for a few seconds and then blow up—which wasn't uncommon—the icy fingers I hated would reach right around my heart. I would

shut my eyes for a brief instant, pray for a little more nerve, and then say to myself, "R-e-l-a-x, you jerk!" My temples would pound, but I would keep my hands flexible and easy of motion and feel. I've heard lots of pilots tell of narrow escapes and say, "Things happened so fast I didn't have time to get scared." I found no matter how fast things happened I always had time to get scared.

A number of the raids were rough enough to keep some of the boys from sleeping at night for sweating out the next one. But, there again, I was lucky. When I got my feet on the ground after one mission, I rarely had trouble sleeping because of the next one. The raids went quickly. That, too, was another factor to help. We didn't have too much time to sit around and think about the next mission. Another thing that helped was

43

"My sack, Corsica, 1944," remembered Joe Kingsbury, a 320th Bomb Group B-26 pilot. All the comforts of home, from bedside canteen to pierced-steel plank (PSP) for a floor. *Joseph S. Kingsbury*

After the 320th Bomb Group got settled on Sardinia in 1944, the officers' club was under construction in no time. With some very talented nose artists in the group, the mural decorations quickly took on the form of desired companions. It wasn't home, but it wasn't bad. *Joseph S. Kingsbury*

44

that we suffered absolutely no limitations of weather. Sometimes the haze was very heavy over the Mediterranean; but the sky was always clear at our base, and we never had to cancel a mission because of cloud over the target.

Bob Gillman
B-24 pilot, 456th Bomb Group

The weather was clear as briefed, as we climbed slowly up to 25,000 feet. Looking down at the detail on the ground, it began to sink in that this was *enemy territory*, and we were heading toward the worst target in the world—the Ploesti oil refinery. The total briefed round trip time was seven hours and twenty-five minutes, and we would be flying tight formation all the way. Ed List saw that I was able to fly good formation from the right seat and asked me to fly a lot. This gave him a break and kept me busy, with

less time to worry about what was happening. Intense and accurate flak was briefed, and some fighter attacks were expected. The Germans knew by now where we were going and would be ready and waiting for us.

The element of fear began to grow within me as we continued onward, and I could see the whole crew beginning to tense up. I had not expected that my "baptism of fire" would begin at this target! But I quickly reasoned, as I would do many times again, that nothing could be changed. There were no choices here but to go on. We had been flying now for about three and a half hours, and it was very cold. Fatigue was becoming noticeable, and we would soon be approaching the target area. Actually, the Ploesti oil refinery complex was spread over many square miles, and individual targets within the complex would be assigned to the various groups. As fear began to grow, I had a fleeting thought about how it must be like to be the enemy on the ground looking up at this armada of hundreds of bombers about to drop thousands of tons of death and destruction down upon them.

The weather today was crystal clear as we pressed on closer and closer. However, there was no way of knowing that there was nothing that could possibly prepare us for what was about to take place. At twenty to twenty-five miles away we could clearly see some weather ahead over the target, as we could see dark clouds forming. This was surely strange, since the weather had been so clear, as it was briefed to be. As we got closer, we could begin to see that something was very strange about the cloud formations. They seemed to be constantly moving! It reminded me of the grand finale at a Fourth of July fireworks, when everything is exploding at once. Then it hit me! *My God, it wasn't clouds at all—but barrage flak!* The Germans knew where we were going, and their radar-controlled 88 and 105mm anti-aircraft guns had our altitude "nailed." So they just kept throwing it up continuously. We were able to see the groups going in

Missouri Mule **heads out with other 320th Bomb Group Marauders on a mission in 1945.**
Joseph S. Kingsbury

The bombs from eighteen B-26 Marauders of the 320th Bomb Group begin to impact on the bridge and approaches of Manjua, Italy, 1944. Though seldom reported, medium bombers like the B-26 flew at low altitude through intense flak to deliver their bombs accurately, as clearly evident here. To get such results, losses were often high. *Joseph S. Kingsbury*

Little friend! An 86th Fighter Group P-47D Thunderbolt escorts a formation of 320th Bomb Group Marauders home, 1945. What a sight! No bomber crewman, even if he did think the fighter boys got all the girls, ever felt so good as when a fighter sidled up to take care of any Luftwaffe intruders. *Joseph S. Kingsbury*

46

ahead of us getting clobbered, with B-24s going down all around. It became instantly obvious to me that by flying large formations of bombers through flak like that, the ones that came out the other side would purely and simply be the *lucky* ones. Skill would have little to do with it.

We touched down at base after seven hours and twenty-five minutes in the air on the nose. The best way to describe my feelings as we got out of the plane was that I was completely drained, both physically and mentally. The thought ran through my brain, "*So this is what it is to fly a combat mission!*"

Bud Abbot
B-17 pilot, 483rd Bomb Group

The P-38s used to really enjoy coming over and buzzing our field, in addition to the big headquarters building. All the guys lived in tents, and all our tents were down in a little meadow, down a little slope from the headquarters building. All the officers' tents were down in one area, and then, over on the other side of the headquarters building, were the enlisted men. The officers' tents were kind of on a little slope and out by themselves. The '38s used to love to come in and buzz our area. They'd come in real low, and then they'd throw it up and blow dust

Sometimes bombers were used to take the brass to appointments within the combat zone—and what brass this is! Generals Dwight D. Eisenhower and Mark Clark talk in front of Ike's B-17 in late 1943, as the Allies were attempting to gain a foothold on the Italian boot. *William J. Skinner*

47

A diverted B-17 ready to help move the 31st Fighter Group to their next field, late 1943. Bombers were often detached to serve as transports when units had to be moved quickly. *William J. Skinner*

all over everything. They created quite a ruckus.

We were unable to get field stoves for our tents, so we were quite chilly at night in the spring. We found a bunch of fifty-gallon drums, cut them in half, turned them upside down, cut a little hole in the front of them, and then buried a number ten can full of gravel and sand in the ground. We scrounged some aluminum tubing off a wrecked airplane, and we had a five-gallon

Jerry can. We put that tubing into the Jerry can, ran it under ground, under the tent floor. We didn't have a floor in our tent; it was just dirt. We ran this tube in there and put it in the can. Then you could open the vent in the five-gallon gas can, and it would run the gasoline into that can. It would run in there and drip on the rocks in the can. When you lit it, you had a fire.

Of course, that would put out some smoke and fumes and stuff, so we found a

The dreaded, deadly German 88mm flak gun. This one at Salerno has a number of American kills marked by white circles on the barrel. The 88 was Germany's most effective flak cannon, with just the right balance of range and punch, capable of reaching right up to the American bomber streams. Flak was by far the most dreaded of enemy weapons, since there was no way to tell if a hit was on the way. At least fighters could be tracked and fired back at. *William J. Skinner*

whole bunch of cast-iron pipe; apparently, they had been planning to lay some water pipe somewhere. It was about, oh, four inches. The filler top on the top of the fifty-gallon drum, that pipe would fit just right over it, so we'd stick the pipe right up through the top of the tent. The only trouble was that the pipes were about twenty-five feet long. So the pipe stuck way up in the air. The smoke and fumes and stuff would go out there. A '38 never hit one of them, but one of our crews was up flying a B-17 on a maintenance hop or something like that with no ammunition, no bombs on board, and decided to come in and buzz the area.

He came in real low, and the ball turret hit one of those smoke stacks. The stack didn't break, but it tumbled, end over end, right over the row of tents, flattening about six or eight of them, plus the one that he hit. Fortunately, everybody was out on a mission and nobody was in any of the tents, so no one got hurt. But the ball turret came off of the airplane and fell over into an olive orchard. The guy that was flying wound up getting court martialed, I think. Everybody was mad at him for a long time, because they came back from a mission, all pooped out and ready to hit the sack, and their tents were laying on the ground! It was quite a mess.

Bob DeGroat
B-24 pilot, 459th Bomb Group

Take a bunch of young fellows who are flying life-and-death combat nearly every

49

A stripped-down combat veteran B-17F at Foggia-Main, Italy, June 1944. Though such tired war-weary planes couldn't be used in combat any more, they served as transports and general "hack" aircraft until so worn out they had to be pushed aside. *Fred E. Bamberger*

Life around the bomber bases in Italy was a continual draw for Fifteenth Air Force crews. The Italian people, though very poor from the ravages of war, were always happy to welcome Americans into their lives, as this 483rd Bomb Group pilot discovers near the base at Sterparone, southeast of Foggia. *James C. Leigh via Mrs. M. M. Leigh/Jim Dietz*

50

day, give them their war toys and tell them to go play, and the exuberance of youth tends to show. Our gunnery missions usually got lower and lower to the surface of the water. The gunners, however, soon learned that bullets ricochet at unpredictable angles off the waves, even back at them, so they cut that short.

Buzzing was always fun, so I had lots of encouragement from the crew. A badge of accomplishment was getting low enough to have water spray on the bomb bay doors.

The Italian fishing boats were fair game. The fishermen would see those four big en-gines bearing down on them, and there would be a mad scramble to let the sails down before the prop wash could blow the boat over as the bomber just cleared the mast. I even saw a few fishermen dive over the side.

I actually only buzzed a fishing boat once. My better judgment returned, and although I loved the sensation of speed from being that low, I left the fishermen to their livelihood. Others were as addicted as I was, and I heard speculation about whether or not it was possible to squeeze a B-24 be-tween the lighthouse and the cliffs at the fa-

A formation of 483rd Bomb Group Forts climb out of Sterparone, Italy, for an attack on Germany. *James C. Leigh via Mrs. M. M. Leigh/Jim Dietz*

Noble Holbert and John McArthur make some repairs at their palatial digs on 759th Squadron officers row at Giulia, near Cerignola, home of the 459th Bomb Group. Yes sir, this was living. Well, at least the tents each had a small stove. *James Wilson via 459th Bomb Group Assn.*

mous spur on the boot of Italy if you banked the plane to ninety degrees. I cannot verify that anyone ever tried.

Lyle McCarty
B-24 pilot, 459th Bomb Group

Weather proved a serious problem off and on during the entire stay of the 459th in Italy—worse, of course, during the winter months. Besides the problem of flying in and out of a field essentially devoid of navigational aids (Giulia Field boasted a nondirectional radio beacon, and that put it a notch

above almost any other field in Italy), the targets were often hidden beneath an undercast. Also, the Germans employed smoke generators to obscure targets, especially oil refineries. To enable the group to strike their targets under these conditions of poor or no visibility, "Mickey" ships were introduced and used for group and squadron lead and sometimes deputy lead aircraft. These planes were radar equipped (the ball turret was replaced by a radome) and carried an additional navigator trained in the use of the Mickey equipment. Bombing accuracy

Liberators of the 459th Bomb Group pulling vapor trails as they climb out of Italy over the Alps for Germany. The group arrived in the theater in January and February 1944 and got a Distinguished Unit Citation for leading the 304th Bomb Wing 23 April 1944 mission through fighters and flak to the aircraft factory at Bad Voslau. *James Wilson via 459th Bomb Group Assn.*

was a bit ragged, but the radar was used quite effectively to establish positions while flying to and from the targets. Mickey craft were originally bare aluminum, but later they were painted a light gray to distinguish them from the other planes.

Ken Kailey
C-47 pilot, 8th Troop Carrier Squadron

I think that troop carrier was just about the best deal in the Army Air Forces. Although the C-47 was not among the "fast and flashy" aircraft, it was solid, dependable, and easy to fly—and so very forgiving. It's still around today, isn't it! While the bombers and fighters did their same old routine each time—fly to 30,000 feet, suck on oxygen for hours, drop the bombs, and re-

Lieutenant Jack Evans, a B-24 pilot with the 759th Squadron, 459th Bomb Group, has just finished shining his shoes . . . on a board . . . in the middle of the mud at Giulia. Now where is he going to go? Why did he bother? *James Wilson via 459th Bomb Group Assn.*

Navigator John D. McArthur and pilot Noble G. Holbert make their way through the mud at Giulia, home of the 459th Bomb Group at Cerignola, Italy. About the only way to beat the stuff was to wear those large flying boots over your shoes, then take off the boots when entering a tent, building, or the airplane. *James Wilson via 459th Bomb Group Assn.*

By the time the Fifteenth Air Force had become firmly established in Italy, the country became another "aircraft carrier" similar to England, as this field full of bombers near Rome clearly shows. *James Wilson via 459th Bomb Group Assn.*

turn to same old field—we had variety. You might say that we were in the Sightseeing Corps. We flew low enough to see things, and we got to land at the other end and look around. Very casual—we were told to fly to point "A," pick up a load, and take it to point "B." No flight plan to file, no assigned altitude. And if we wanted to stray off course a bit to check something out, no problem. Besides that, they weren't shooting at us all the time.

We pretty much covered the European theater—I got to visit France, London, Casablanca, Cairo, Athens, and most of the major cities in Italy. In addition, we viewed most of the points in between from the air. And the most thankful part of all is that I'm still here today!

Bob DeGroat
B-24 pilot, 459th Bomb Group

Before we had our own plane, a B-24G called *Cherry II*, we were usually assigned Number 614, a B-24J. Unfortunately, it had a balky number three engine that was difficult to start. Several times it caused us to be

A 759th Squadron, 459th Bomb Group, Ford-built B-24M waits on its PSP hardstand at Giulia in 1944 for the next mission. The four-leaf clover on the nose was one of the squadron's symbols, carried on several Liberators. *James Wilson via 459th Bomb Group Assn.*

Patches **was another of the 459th Bomb Group's veteran Liberators. She survived the war and made it back to Altus, Oklahoma, only to be scrapped.** *Claude Porter via 459th Bomb Group Assn.*

real late, requiring "cleaning up" on the move, although we never missed our proper order in the procession. Semi-humorously, our copilot named the engines after former girlfriends according to how hard they were to get started.

Philip Ardery
B-24 squadron commander, 389th Bomb Group

When a group lost heavily on one or two raids, there was a natural strain on the morale of the remaining combat crews. It was hard for the boys coming back to go to quarters that were practically vacant—quarters that had been full a few hours before. It wore on their nerves to go to the club and find the place more filled with the ghosts of those who had gone than the presence of the few who remained. General Doolittle was a savvy guy about this particular hardship. I heard a story about a visit

A 489th Squadron, 340th Bomb Group B-25J at Capodocino, Naples, November 1944. The 340th had been decimated by the eruption of Mt. Vesuvius but came back strong to maintain its place as one of the theater's most effective medium bomb groups. Originally attached to the Ninth Air Force in North Africa, the group transferred to the Twelfth Air Force and continued to hit tactical targets through the end of the war. *Fred E. Bamberger*

he made to one of the groups that had lost nearly everyone on a single raid. The incident happened just after the unit had been filled up with replacements following a similar occurrence only a few weeks before. The general, as was his custom, flew his own fighter plane to the base and went unannounced to pay a visit to the officers club.

It was late evening, and the bar was open. A lone lieutenant was solemnly drinking a beer. The general stepped up beside him and ordered one. The lieutenant, noticing who the newcomer was, turned to the star-bearing little flyer and said, "What're you doing up here, General? Lookin' over our morale?"

The general smiled. "Not at all. I try to get around to visit all my groups every now and then. I didn't have much to do in headquarters this afternoon, so I decided I'd fly up and pay you a call."

"You know, General," the lieutenant continued, "Funny thing, morale. Ours is okay till the high-ranking generals start coming around lookin' it over. Then it just goes all to hell."

The general laughed, chatted with the officer a while, went out, climbed in his ship, and flew off. Yes, General Doolittle was a savvy guy. He was hard when the situation called for that, but when he left that group that day he knew that there was enough

A veteran 484th Bomb Group B-24 on the way out of Torretto, another of the Fifteenth Air Force Liberator bases near Cerignola. The group got two Distinguished Unit Citations. They earned the first on 13 June 1944 for hitting the marshaling yards at Innsbruck after a heavy smoke screen prevented dropping on the primary target at Munich. The second citation honored their 21 August 1944 bombing of Vienna without fighter escort. *Lieutenant Colonel J. Pool via David W. Menard*

fighting spirit in the handful of flying men left to give proper inspiration to the new bunch of replacements he was sending in.

Bob DeGroat
B-24 pilot, 459th Bomb Group

I remember one occasion being overloaded with six 1,000-pound bombs instead of the usual ten 500-pounders. On another we had to take off downwind. Power lines diagonally crossing that end of the runway forced me to bank and fly down them until I had enough altitude to clear. The tower wisely decided to change the direction of takeoff after three of us had problems. We circled the field while the whole bomb group reassembled at the other end of the runway.

Jim Bakewell
B-24 nose turret gunner, 459th Bomb Group

In August 1944, as a nose turret gunner on a mission over Blechhammer, Germany, I had something happen to me that never happened on any of my other missions. On the bomb run with very rough flak, at approximately the time for "bombs away," I suddenly had an extremely intense urge to urinate. There was no way to wait until we had pulled off the target; I had to do it immediately. With great effort, I stood up with my five-foot-eleven frame hunched up against the Plexiglas roof and doubled over in a "half-moon" shape. With greater effort, I extracted my "apparatus" through my heavy

Headquarters, Twelfth Air Force, Peretola, Italy, November 1944. Many war weary bombers ended up as headquarters hacks, stripped of armament. This early model "clean" B-25 sits next to a newer B-25J of the 321st Bomb Group. *Fred E. Bamberger*

flying suit and flak jacket (I still don't know how I did so), and I proceeded to make a "direct hit" on the Plexiglas covering the front of my turret. All hell was breaking loose outside our plane, but I didn't care about the flak or anything else. I had to do what I had to do. As I settled back down into my seat, I figured the bombardier would "chew me out," but he never said a word. I discovered that the fluid had frozen on the Plexiglas, and apparently he never saw what happened.

When we landed and were standing outside of our plane, eating doughnuts and drinking coffee served by the Red Cross girls, an armorer or crew chief came along and said, "Who is the nose turret gunner on this plane?" I admitted that I was and walked with him to look at the turret per his request. He said, "What in the hell are those stains on the Plexiglas?" I said that I didn't know, but suggested that maybe we hit a bird on the way in for landing, and that caused the stains. He said, "The stains are not on the outside, but inside." I replied that I had absolutely no idea what could have caused such an amazing thing. It was my suggestion that he talk to the bombardier and see if he knew anything about it. Whether the armorer or crew chief ever did so, I do not know, but just in case he remembers this episode after forty years, I confess that I was the culprit.

Bob DeGroat
B-24 pilot, 459th Bomb Group

I always felt sorry for the copilot. The first pilot invariably had the controls on the bomb run and was, therefore, occupied. The copilot, on the other hand, had very little to do but watch the flak and enemy fighters. Unless your box was leading the Fifteenth Air Force formation, the surprise for the enemy as to our target for the day was over, and the copilot could see the intense flak curtain that we would eventually have to go through (no matter where we went in the sky first). Those minutes must have seemed

59

The ground crew of a 460th Bomb Group Liberator readies bombs for the next mission at Spinazzola, south of Cerignola, Italy. The group got a Distinguished Unit Citation for leading the 55th Bomb Wing through adverse weather and heavy enemy fire to bomb the airfield and aircraft repair facilities at Zwolfaxing, Austria, on 26 July 1944. *USAF*

like hours. The copilot may have been the bravest man on any bomber crew.

A. H. Albrecht
B-25 pilot, 319th Bomb Group

I was fortunate enough to fly twenty-five B-26 and six A-26 missions in addition to twenty in the B-25—which was much easier to fly than either of the others. I flew my first B-25 combat mission with a total time of 100 hour's training, but I never felt comfortable with a B-26 till I had 300 hours of first-pilot time. The B-25J was much easier to fly on one engine; the B-26 barely flew on one, but the A-26 did nicely. Takeoff and landing were easy by comparison with the B-26, and formation flying was easier in the Mitchell than either of the others. The B-26 was the hardest to fly but the most rugged. The A-26 was a superb airplane—same bomb load as the others but forty miles per

hour faster; two or three man crew; single-engine performance exceptional. The B-25 had no problems with oil coolers (the B-26 was bad in this way) and none with propellers, whereas the B-26's propellers could run away. The B-25's Wright Cyclone engines were much noisier than the Pratt & Whitneys in the other two, and the B-25 had much less room everywhere than the B-26.

Philip Ardery
B-24 squadron commander, 389th Bomb Group

Part of my reaction to my luck and general combat experience was to sense a resurgence of religion. Fellows who hadn't attended services in years found themselves going to Sunday services. My religion didn't take me to these services with regularity, but I went occasionally, not only for myself but to let the men in my squadron know I

Headquarters, Twelfth Air Force, Peretola, Florence, Italy, on VE-Day, May 1945. The conglomeration of bombers, fighters, trainers, and transports made the place more than interesting, particularly for headquarters pilots who wanted a variety of flying time. *Fred E. Bamberger*

didn't consider attendance a sign of weakness. I felt if they saw me there it might help some of them to go who wanted to but were kept from going out of embarrassment.

In my case, religion made me say short prayers before going to sleep at night and sometimes during a fleeting instant at the height of combat. I think this undoubtedly made me a better combat officer. It comforted me so that I could sleep before missions, even though I had been briefed for the next mission and knew the assignment of the morning might be my last. It helped me to say to myself with complete calm: "You can't live forever. You have had a great deal in your life span already, much more than many people ever have. You would not shirk the duty tomorrow if you could. Go into it calmly; don't try too hard to live. Don't ever give up hope; never let the fear of death

strike panic in your mind and paralyze your reason. Death will find you sometime, if not tomorrow. Give yourself a chance." And then I would remember that very appropriate sentence of Shakespeare: "Cowards die many times before their deaths; the valiant never taste of death but once."

Bob Gillman
B-24 pilot, 456th Bomb Group

I am in a state of euphoria, since this is my last mission, and each of the crew have been joking about how nice it would be if I would volunteer to fly additional missions until they are finished too. Fat chance! I feel as though an enormous weight has just been lifted from my back, and it's really hard to believe that I will not be flying any more combat missions. What a thrill to bring the

A 450th Bomb Group Liberator on takeoff at Florence, April 1945. The 450th was based at Manduria, east of Taranto, as a part of the 47th Bomb Wing. Though the Liberator was often overshadowed by its more famous stable mate, the B-17, the type was built in larger numbers (more than 18,000) than any other American aircraft. *Fred E. Bamberger*

formation over the field for the last time, peeling off in turn and landing.

After evening chow, I invite the crew to come to our tent for a few drinks to join me in celebrating my final mission. I must also remember to write to my family tonight to give them the good news. I am sure that this great feeling will be with me for quite a while. I have not even begun to think about what my plans will be, except that I will be able to spend more time with my extracurricular flying activities. It is such a great feeling and a great relief not to be aroused at 0530 in the morning to fly another mission, but, strangely, I feel just a twinge of guilt. I am concerned about my crew having to fly

with someone else, and I sweat them out each mission until they return.

Ralph "Doc" Watson
wing commander, Fifteenth Air Force
    Italy 0730 P.M.
    Thanksgiving Day
    November 23, 1944
    Dear Little Sis,

I only wish that I could be there with you tonite to comfort you, instead of having to write you from thousands of miles away. I will try and tell you all I can.

I was notified last night of Gordon's death. Early this morning, I got into my Mustang and flew down to his base.

A 450th Bomb Group B-24 taxies out at Florence, April 1945. The flight engineer is at the top hatch to help guide the pilots on the ground, a normal procedure across the Army Air Forces. *Fred E. Bamberger*

I got in touch with Lieutenant Sanderson, Sergeant Spindle, and Sergeant Nelson, who had been with Gordon and who had successfully bailed out. The rest of the crew didn't get out. The accident happened yesterday morning at about eight o'clock. I talked with the squadron doctor and the three boys for a long time, finding out all of the details that I could. When the ship hit, Gordon was thrown clear but was badly broken up and died instantly. All three of the boys landed nearby in their parachutes and a few seconds later everybody was taken to the hospital.

When I got down to the field this morning, they were having the funeral at the American Cemetery for the Fifteenth Air Force fliers. Gordon was buried in Plot L, Row 12, Grave 1723. Chaplain Golden, the group chaplain, conducted the services. The chaplain had gone down from the group. The caskets were draped with the American flag, and it was a beautiful little cemetery with an American flag waving over all. I knelt down by myself and prayed to God over Gordon's grave.

They informed me that the bodies would be sent back to America after the war

if you so desire. I have the location, and all the graves are well marked with concrete markers.

I then saluted the flag and went back to the field and flew back to his group. There, I gathered up Gordon's personal things and brought them back here with me. I will send them to you in a little box—the rest will be sent home by the army. I am enclosing his ring in this letter; he had it on when they crashed. His bracelet and his Bible, which he had with him, are in the box with your letters and pictures.

Midge, honey, my heart goes out to you, and I cannot begin to express my feelings and sympathy by this letter. I only hope that you will take it like a good flier's wife, which you are, and be proud, knowing that Gordon died as a hero fighting for his country, and that the little boys and girls now growing up may enjoy the freedom and privileges which America is fighting for. I know that you loved him dearly, Midge, and I know that he lived and breathed for you. It is God's will, Margaret, and I pray to Him that you will be strong. God bless you always, my dear little sweet sister.

Words seem so futile, but I will always be where you may lean on my shoulders, God willing.

Always, your brother,
Ralph

Fresh from the States, these brand new B-24s lined up, ready for assignment to a bomb group, at Capodocino, Naples, in November 1944. At this point in the war, American industry was building aircraft at such a furious rate that these new aircraft were often stored. Replacement had finally overtaken combat losses, something unheard of earlier in the war. *Fred E. Bamberger*

A 450th Bomb Group B-24M, built at Ford's Willow Run plant, taxies out at Florence in April 1944. The group began combat operations with the Fifteenth Air Force in January 1944, going straight into "Big Week" over Germany in February and winning a Distinguished Unit Citation in the process for pressing through bad weather, fighters, and flak to get bombs on target. *Fred E. Bamberger*

An Army Air Forces OA-10A Catalina at Foggia, May 1945. There was no more wonderful sight than one of these "Dumbos" coming in to pick up a crew that had ditched at sea. Often unheralded, Army Catalina crews braved some of the most intense enemy fire to rescue airmen in distress. *Fred E. Bamberger*

The Flight Section, Headquarters Twelfth Air Force, Peretola Field, Florence, Italy, May 1945. Yep, this was all there was. A working, moving air force rarely had time to build fine buildings or worry about the comforts of home. If this got the job done, then why waste time building anything more complicated? *Fred E. Bamberger*

Officers of the 344th Bomb Group watch with detached curiosity as a caravan weighs in at the scales outside the walls of Medina, Morocco. Such diversion was a welcome respite from the tents these men lived at their field in Marrakech while waiting to depart for England, March 1944. *Jack K. Havener*

CHAPTER 3

Life in the ETO

Sam Wilson
ground echelon, 17th Bomb Group (letter home, October 1942)

I'm sorry I can't tell you . . . when we first arrived, how we traveled and where we are. However, I can say that England is really beautiful—everything is so neat and orderly. The trains are just like in the movies—only no sleeping accommodations except luxury trains, no dining cars. Sunday we visited Cambridge, which is quaint—no buildings are over three stories. The streets are cobblestone and run in every damned direction! The lower-class English rather resent us; however, the middle class and upper bend over backwards being nice to us.

We are at one of the finest airdromes; the accommodations are excellent. In fact they beat those of my former station. Virginia creeper, ivy, and honeysuckle grow on many of the structures, and there are lawns, roses, and poplars. A few observations on the customs. We're taking to "tea" wonderfully . . . the Bank of England (Lloyds?) representative changed our money. I can't make

change yet; they have a god-awful system.

The Scotch people we have met are really swell, more like Yanks.

We have to watch our slang. Have already had a few misunderstandings that way.

The British version of toilet tissue is equivalent to the rotogravure section of the Sears Roebuck catalogue. There are no oranges. We will soon be eating American food tho' I like English food, but they have tried to cook our dishes and have flopped so far. But their hospitality extended that far!

The English people have taken a terrible beating in the air raids, and many people show it. When they play, they play hard, though they have very high spirits and rarely speak of the war except in passing, or else of the end of it. They have no doubts as to an English victory.

The British WAAFs [Women's Army Air Force] are taken very seriously and do a good job. We paled up with a few at a pub, and they knew our latest songs and some slang. . . . the English seem to feel that our

High Street and the town square, Diss, the village closest to the 100th Bomb Group at Thorpe Abbots, East Anglia. These old towns, particularly their pubs, became hubs of activity for Americans. *Arnold N. Delmonico*

When the Army Air Forces "invaded" England, many units were based near the food-providing farms (so crucial for the war effort) that dotted the nation. Here, the 322nd Bomb Group's Marauders nestle next to Bacon Farm, Stebbing, September 1943. The group was the first to fly B-26s from Britain, beginning 14 May 1943. *USAF*

A train pulls into the station at Eye where a few Americans wait to board. Such weather was the norm rather than the exception. *Arnold N. Delmonico*

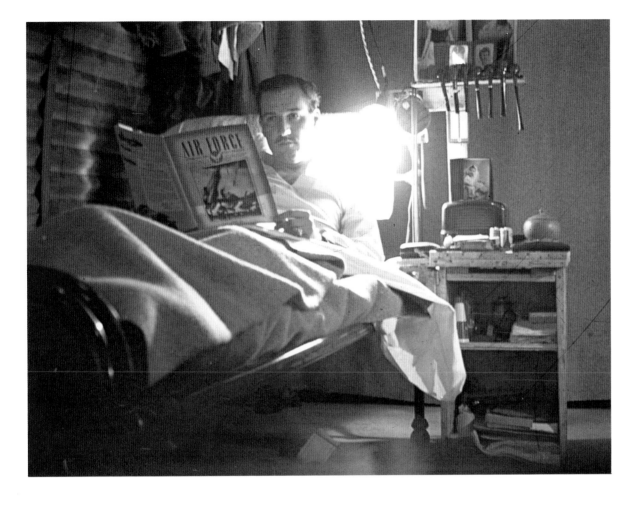

Ninth Air Force Marauder pilot Jack Havener in his sack at Stanstead, just north of Bishops Stortford, home of the 344th Bomb Group from March through September 1944. This was livin', brother . . . and that was no joke, particularly compared to the tents, mud, and grit of most other theaters of war. *Jack K. Havener*

high pay will buy up everything in the way of luxuries; one British major said to me that if we kept drinking at the rate we were (really very little on American standards) all the Scotch in England would be gone in a month! So you can see, we are rightly called "crazy Yanks" (they call us Yanks whatever we are).

The blackouts are terrific, 100 percent all over. I've bumped into lampposts a hundred times and said politely "beg your pardon."

In conclusion, I'm well, I'm happy. . . . I like the country, the people, and a fraction of the customs.

If you send a package, make it the size of a shoe box. I'd like some pine nuts, stamps, and airmail stationery. I'll write soon again.

All my love,
Sam

Ben Smith

B-17 radio operator, 303rd Bomb Group

We were hardly down and checked in before our new airplane was taken away from us, never to be seen again. This was quite a shock, especially to Bachman. We had even named the airplane. Our morale took a nose-dive. For the first time, the realization

A cross-country jaunt across the English farmland, full of railroad crossings like this one at a country rail station. *Mark Brown/USAFA*

began to steal over us that we were not something special. We were not Chick's Crew—we were "fresh meat," replacements, soon to be gobbled up by the voracious appetite of the air war like all those who had gone before. A chill rain was falling. We huddled together dejectedly, full of gloomy foreboding.

John Gabay
B-17 tail gunner, 94th Bomb Group

When we came back from a raid, usually between 4:00 and 5:00 P.M., we were picked up by a truck or jeep and brought to the interrogation shack. After that, to the mess hall for chow, then to the armament shack to clean our guns. We got back to the barracks between 8:00 and 9:00 P.M., exhausted. My raids averaged eight hours and forty minutes in the air. So when we finally got back to our barracks, the thing uppermost in our minds was to crawl into the sack and go to sleep.

Although a war was in progress, as far

as we were concerned, everything centered around our barracks. It was located at the very end of the base, surrounded by woods in the back and open fields in the front. The base road ended at our front door. Across the road were the washroom and showers. A perfect setup. When the truck came to pick us up for a raid, it had to turn around in the fields. Directly across the fields (about 200 yards) was a tar road. If you went left on the road for about two miles, you ended up in the town of Bury St. Edmunds. But if you went right for about a mile, you hit an Eng-

lish pub, standing out in the middle of nowhere. When we were sure there wasn't a raid the next day, we drew straws to see who would go to the pub for a barracks bag full of bottled beer. The same guy always drew the short straw, and he never caught on. It was no easy task coming back with a sack full of beer—and riding a bicycle. If he broke a bottle or two, which he occasionally did, everyone would bawl him out, and the poor guy would always apologize. A few months later he was shot down, and we all missed him. Not because we loved him, but because we

Regardless of wartime pressures and bombing raids, Piccadilly Circus remained a flurry of activity, both day and night, attracting Americans based across the United Kingdom. *Byron Trent*

73

Maintenance area, 94th Bomb Group, Bury St. Edmunds. Nissen huts and large, freestanding hangars were easy to build and dotted Eighth Air Force fields in England like runaway weeds. Though such temporary structures were cursed for letting in so much of the cold and wet English weather, they were far better than the tents that typically housed Ninth Air Force groups. *Byron Trent*

The 333rd Bomb Squadron living area at Bury St. Edmunds, 1944. Nissen huts were cold and drafty, and it was amazing how attached one could get to a coal-burning pot-bellied stove. *Byron Trent*

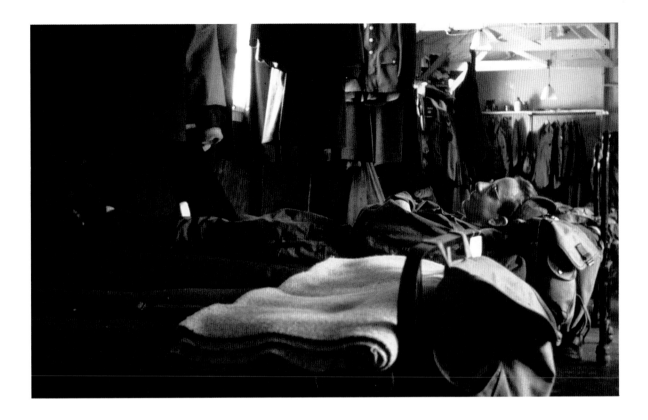

would have to look for another live one. The next day we got six new rookies so we made sure one of them always got the short straw—and they never found out. Hard to believe!

Some nights when we were drinking beer, one of the comedians would drink a toast to the guys who were shot down. It was always a comical takeoff of an old World War I movie. It would start out very solemn, and then turn into a roast—especially if the guys didn't leave any cigarettes or candy in their foot lockers. What really cracked us up was when the clown giving the toast couldn't remember the names of the guys being toasted. Not very good copy for a movie or the folks back home, but that's the way it was— no dramatics, no sadness, no hearts and flowers.

John Ramsey
B-17 navigator, 493rd Bomb Group

In 1938, I began to write to a pen-friend, Miss Joan Green, in Leeds, Yorkshire. After a year or two we lost contact. However, Joan's address stayed somewhere in the back of my mind, and after I arrived in the United Kingdom and became settled in at Debach in September 1944, I wrote Joan, knowing she probably wondered what had become of me as the war unfolded. She and her mother both wrote back urging me to come to Leeds at the first opportunity. There was much hesitation because I knew about rationing in England, besides which the rail connections were very vague. There were no regular advertised schedules, probably for security reasons. I finally decided to give it a try, and, after the first time, made the trip

Captain John Meyers
in the 386th Bomb
Group chow tent at St.
Trond, Belgium, early
1945. When the Ninth
Air Force moved to the
Continent in late 1944,
it left behind all
vestiges of real
comfort. Few groups
had more than tents to
begin with. Life in the
field was a series of
quick moves and
constant bad weather.
John H. Meyers

frequently, but I never got to Leeds by the same route twice! When I boarded the train at Ipswich, it was with the understanding that the conductor would tell me where to get off to make the first connection. Then in the next station I'd ask someone which train to get on, and the next conductor would tell me where to get off again, and so on to Leeds.

On one occasion in the bitter cold winter of 1944–45, I had an interesting encounter.

It was so cold that at each stop I would buy a cup of tea and two or three of those hard little cookies or crackers. The tea wasn't just to drink—by holding the cup between my hands I could warm them, as there was no heating in the carriages. On one leg of the journey I found myself in a compartment with a young Royal Air Force sergeant. His insignia indicated he was an aircrew member, and I immediately felt that I had a friend. However, I tried without success to

In spite of the usual rough living conditions, there were times when a dream came true. After living in tents up through the Mediterranean, the officers of the 320th Bomb Group were assigned this chateau at Longecourt, France, in early 1945. *Joseph S. Kingsbury*

77

Unfortunately, the 340th Bomb Group enlisted men had to pitch their tents in the snow and ice behind the officers' chateau at Longecourt. Army life never seemed to be fair for noncoms, a fate most endured with resignation.
Joseph S. Kingsbury

A local resident near the base at Eye, England, trades some good-natured conversation with one of the 490th Bomb Group's pilots. Though the common description of the Yanks was "overpaid, oversexed, and over here," for the most part, the Americans and the British got along very well.
Arnold N. Delmonico

strike up conversation. He would only answer my questions with a very curt "yes" or "no." At the next station we both changed trains, and I heard him mention that he was going to the Bradford area. I knew Bradford was near Leeds, so I stuck to the young sergeant like wallpaper—you better believe I was having a hard time with the English accents trying to understand directions.

When we set off again there was an older man sitting opposite us in the compartment who noticed my attempts to engage the Royal Air Force sergeant in conversation. He explained that British enlisted personnel do not converse with officers except

to answer questions and then as briefly as possible. This older man then pointed out to the young sergeant that the Yank was trying to be friendly and that he, the sergeant, was not being properly polite. The Royal Air Force man relaxed after that and was soon all smiles. He proved to be as curious about the Eighth Air Force as I was about Royal Air Force Bomber Command.

He was a Lancaster gunner and had completed a tour of duty but was hoping that his pilot could pull a few strings so that he could remain on operations. He felt that if he was grounded he might end up in "the pits," the coal mines, which I assume was his

Buzz job! A 379th Bomb Group Fort clips the grass at Mt. Farm to give the 7th Photo Group boys something to talk about. Though strictly prohibited, and not a little dangerous, buzzing was considered great sport among all Army pilots, particularly at the finish of a combat tour. *Robert Astrella*

Sick bay, 65th US Army General Hospital. Eighth Air Force personnel used these hospitals with alarming frequency. *Arnold N. Delmonico*

peacetime job. He was fascinated by our going to targets in broad daylight while I couldn't imagine milling around in darkness in the midst of other aircraft. We talked about how interesting it would be to trade places for one mission.

As the journey wore on, it became apparent that at the rate of progress we were making I was not going to arrive in Leeds until two or three o'clock in the morning. I asked if anyone in the compartment might recommend a hotel close to the rail station. Immediately a woman said that there should be no need to find a hotel as she was sure that any householder to whom I explained my predicament would be happy to find me a bed for the night, further suggesting that when I got to Leeds I should "knock someone up." I was momentarily taken

aback by this statement, as in American slang it means making someone pregnant. This was the first time I had heard this expression from a Britisher but quickly realized that the woman was telling me to go bang on a door.

At the same time my newfound Royal Air Force friend invited me to go home with him if I didn't mind getting off at Bradford, taking a bus with him to a smaller place, and walking a mile. He pressed me, but I had to decline. I knew how few rations these people got. For example, my friends the Greens had nine people in their home and could only buy two eggs a week. I was also aware that the sergeant's family was not aware he was coming on leave, and I could picture the scene when he arrived unexpectedly in the wee hours with a Yank in tow. His offer was appreciated more than he probably realized, but I begged off on the grounds that my leave time was too short, which was true.

That night was spent at the Queens Hotel, an act for which Mrs. Green scolded me soundly when I arrived next day. Felt badly about the Royal Air Force man's offer as I probably hurt his feelings in declining. I wish I had gotten his name and address, and I often wonder if he survived the air war.

Bob Morgan
B-17 pilot, 91st Bomb Group

When we went overseas, the British built these temporary fields for us. On a practice mission we tore the runway all to pieces, so we couldn't use it, and were grounded until we found another place to go. Our group commander, Colonel Wray, was a very versatile person who was able to do a lot of things. He heard about this base at Bassingbourn, an old British permanent base with brick houses and all the fineries near the town of Royston. He went down to visit it on his own without permission from

One of the Eighth's early 97th Bomb Group veterans, a B-17E, JW-M, now turned into a war-weary hack for the 92nd Bomb Group. Stripped of armament and combat equipment, the Fort was almost like a fighter to fly when compared to a '17 at full gross weight. *Robert Astrella*

81

After being transferred to the 92nd Bomb Group at Bovingdon, this B-17E introduced crews to the procedures on in-theater combat flying. It then made its way around as a staff transport, ending up with the 100th Bomb Group. *Robert Astrella*

the higher command, and there was nobody using it. He went back to the base and moved us down there without any orders! General Eaker found out about it, and Colonel Wray nearly got court martialed, but they finally said, "You're there. All right, stay there." We ended up with the best base in England, no question about it, living pretty high on the hog.

Jack Havener
B-26 pilot, 344th Bomb Group

"How's the ankle this morning, Lieutenant?" The GI medic was all smiles as he brought me a cup of coffee and the morning *London Daily Express*. I told him it was still throbbing, but as long as I kept it elevated, it wasn't so bad. I was in the small base hospital of the 344th Bomb Group (M) at Stansted-Mountfichet, Essex, England, recuperating from a flak wound received the

day before. Sipping the coffee, I leafed through the *Express*, looking for some news of our mission. All I could find was an article on the third page:

FORTS AND LIBS ON BIG STRIKE

21 June 1944—Over 1,000 Flying Fortresses and Liberators of the U.S. Eighth Air Force struck telling blows on Hitler's Germany yesterday. Factories and strategic targets deep within the Reich were pounded with tons of high explosives and incendiaries in the continuing air battle. Walls of flak were encountered and the Luftwaffe put up a tremendous defensive effort with all types of fighter aircraft. The Eighth Fighter Command reported fourteen enemy fighters knocked down to only three lost in the more than four hundred of our planes escorting the bombers. Twenty-eight bombers failed to return to their home bases

As in no era before or since, aircraft nose art was the hallmark of World War II, as *Lilly Ann* demonstrates. Aircraft in the European Theater of Operations were graced by nose art of all forms, on all types of aircraft, but the bomber was the ideal canvas. *Robert Astrella*

after the raids but the gallant airmen of the Eighth are already preparing for another strike tomorrow. Mediums of the Ninth Air Force were also out.

"Mediums were also out!" I exclaimed to a navigator in the next bed. "Why in the hell does the Eighth get all the recognition? We're in this war too!" Shifting his weight off his bandaged hip he replied, "Hell's fire, Johnny, don't you know? They've got Clark Gable and Jimmy Stewart on their team!"

Ben Smith
B-17 radio operator, 303rd Bomb Group

There was almost no distinction between officers and noncoms. The lowest grade on a crew was staff sergeant. Often the bombardier was a noncommissioned officer. The officers and men went on pass together and chummed with each other. There was not much saluting or military formality except in formations held for decorations or visiting dignitaries. An officer in charge of our squadron was called the ground CO [commanding officer] or adjutant. He managed to stay drunk most of the time. He didn't bother us, and we didn't bother him. I recall only one inspection of the barracks while I was there. I don't know what prompted that one.

We seldom wore uniforms. Our dress

83

Alice Blue Gown **was indeed a lovely lady, managing to take her crews through sixty-seven missions with the 851st Squadron, 490th Bomb Group, out of Eye.** *Arnold N. Delmonico*

was flight coveralls and leather A-2 jackets. We clomped around a lot in our flight boots, always when we went to the latrine or some short distance, because they were warm. We either went bareheaded or wore the leather fleece-lined gunners' caps. I can recall wearing my flight coveralls for days at a time without taking them off. I would sleep in them too. We cleaned our ODs [wool uniforms] in aviation gas. Consequently, we smelled like gasoline when we were dressed up to go on pass.

If we wanted to take a shower, we had to go a considerable distance to the showers. There was never any hot water. It was just too much trouble and a very punishing experience, so nobody bothered. Sponge baths had to do. After a time we couldn't smell ourselves; or we thought we smelled all right, because everybody else smelled that way.

We had a few English radios that were continually malfunctioning. The BBC was dry as dust; the Armed Forces Network was what we listened to. The AFN was the best link we had to home as they played a lot of good jazz, featuring the big name bands of that era. We listened to Axis Sally a lot. She would call some guy's name in the 92nd Bomb Group and tell him his wife was dating a lot. It probably was the truth. We

thought these little gems were funny as hell; they delighted us to no end. Far from damaging our morale, these broadcasts from the enemy were a source of great pleasure to us.

Each crewman had his favorite pinups on the wall behind his bunk. These were highly prized and usually came from *Yank* magazine. The favorites were Betty Grable, Chili Williams in the two-piece polka dot bathing suit, and Rita Hayworth in a silk negligee—the picture that was in *Life* magazine. Sometimes the movie stars sent autographed photos in response to requests. I had one of Ginger Rogers that she had signed. A friend gave it to me. I still have it. I never saw a lewd picture as this was before pornography killed off the pinup.

In the barracks there was a never-ending poker game. George Kepics, our ball turret gunner, was always a big winner. Every month or so he would send home nearly a thousand dollars. He was a rich man when the war was over. We warned the other guys, but they would play with him anyway. The problem was that George was a pro, and they were a bunch of turkeys. There was al-

ways a Shylock in every squadron, and most of the guys stayed in hock to him, mostly because of George. The Shylock's interest rates would have shocked any loan shark back in the States. Of course, if the Shylock went down, all debts were paid, but there was always another to take his place.

Paradoxically, our tenuous existence had the effect of ridding us of the twin sins of covetousness and avarice. The men on the combat crews were completely unselfish. They shared everything—nothing else would have made sense. When someone got a box from home, it was opened right on the spot and shared by all. Nothing was hoarded except whiskey. We loved for the Jewish boys to get boxes from home, because theirs were the best—full of salami, knockwurst, gefiltefisch, pumpernickel, bagels, kosher dills, and all kinds of great things from the "deli," plus the inevitable Manischewitz. The flight crews were also generous with their English friends, sharing an endless booty of chewing gum, chocolates, silk hose, and cigarettes with them. A few boorish fellows attempted to use these goodies to bargain for

Traffic at Mt. Farm. One of the 92nd Bomb Group's B-17E hacks runs up prior to takeoff as the 7th Photo Group control jeep heads back to the line and a visiting Royal Air Force pilot walks in from his de Havilland Dominie. *Robert Astrella*

A 490th Bomb Group Fort, *Love 'em All*, on takeoff at Eye, late 1944. The basis of the nose art was copied from the Alberto Vargas July 1943 *Esquire* magazine gatefold. Copies of this art ended up on literally hundreds of aircraft before the war was over. *Albert N. Delmonico*

the favors of the English girls, but only the most insensitive ones responded to such degrading behavior. When I was in England in 1977, many people would come up and say, "I was one of the little kids who begged chewing gum from the Yanks through the fence."

No one really cared about money. It was completely irrelevant to our existence. When a crew was going on pass, the hat was passed, and everyone would throw in a few pounds. The crew would have a sizable pot to leave with but would return to base without a cent. The Shylock preyed upon these improvident chaps. Really he was very necessary. Since I didn't care for poker, I sent $100 home every month to be saved for me. I don't know why I was saving it. I didn't think I would ever get to spend it. When I came back to the States, a small fortune awaited me.

One function always well attended was sick call. It was not that the fellows were sick; it was the delightful medicine they served: terpinhydrate, called by its aficionados "GI Gin." It was cough syrup with

codeine in it. A guy could get bombed with a couple of swallows. There was always a long line with a lot of phony coughing going on.

Lalli Coppinger
Red Cross Club volunteer hostess

Maybe, in our ignorance, we in Britain had expected Americans to be more like ourselves. After all, didn't they speak the same language—more or less—and didn't they used to be British? A little World War II British guidebook on "Meeting the Americans" reminded us that they had also once fought a war to get away from us, and although they might not be thought of exactly as foreigners, the little book explained that they certainly weren't another kind of Englishman either!

Getting to know the Americans was a memorable highlight of the war. They provided excitement and brought fun back into our lives at the time we most needed it, when we were suffering greatly from the deprivations of the years of war. They livened up our dreary towns and introduced a new world to us.

We learned to understand each other's cultural differences, but were also surprised to find out how much alike we were in many ways. When we opened up our homes and hospitality to them, they responded wholeheartedly and gradually became a very large part of our lives. Many were in England for as long as three years, plenty of time to form a special bonding and lasting friendships.

The GIs had a great liking for children, who needed no encouragement to make their acquaintance. Their faces would light up when their American friends dug down into their pockets and brought out never-ending supplies of candy and chewing gum. No one will ever forget the catch phrase, "Any gum, chum?"

Bob Morgan
B-17 pilot, 91st Bomb Group

Though I flew the airplane, the rest I left up to the other nine members, and they did a great job. And the tenth and eleventh member: my crew chief. I couldn't tell you a nut from a bolt as far as a B-17 is concerned. All I knew was when she would fly, what she would do, what I could do with her, and what she would do for me. And fortunately enough, what she could do was one of the reasons I lived through it. Some others were not so fortunate.

The Army Air Forces decided to make a documentary of combat, which ended up being named *Memphis Belle* after our airplane. The main purpose was to send it back to the people in the United States and show them what was going on in Europe at that time since this was very early in our participation in World War II. There was a great deal of controversy about the B-17 being able to do the job that the Army Air Forces thought it could do, particularly with men like Eighth Air Force commander General Ira Eaker. There were strong feelings that it couldn't be done. The British pooh-poohed us. They said that there was no way that you could go out and daylight bomb with that airplane or any other airplane and not have casualties so high that it would not be profitable or the net results beneficial.

I must say for the first three or four

months I was there I was kind of questioning myself whether it could be done. We had to learn the hard way. There were no books or training in the United States, except how to fly the airplane, that told us exactly what we had to do. Every mission we learned, and we started to write the manual for combat flying over Europe. It was tough. We lost eighty-two percent of our group in the first three months. When you start looking at those figures, you realize how fortunate we were, and how fortunate I was to live through it. It was rough, but we learned, and, little by little, the job got done.

Memphis Belle was made by the famous movie director William Wyler, who did some great movies, including *Mrs. Miniver* and *The Best Years of Our Lives*. He knew what he was doing as far as shooting film, but he had never been in a position where they were shooting back at him! He flew five mis-

Warner Brothers had its most famous cartoon character painted on a number of aircraft, including this 490th Bomb Group B-17. The aggressive, wisecracking rabbit with the New York accent seemed to be a perfect representation of how aggressive Army aircrews viewed themselves. Cockiness was an integral part of remaining sane through an insane war in which the odds of surviving a combat tour were low. *Albert N. Delmonico*

Staff Sergeant Vern Woodward, a waist gunner with the 97th Bomb Group, is a long way from Greenwich, New York—and he doesn't look all that happy about it. Though this kind of hands-on training could be boring and uncomfortable, particularly if they left you in the Channel for a while, it proved essential. Coming down in the water was dreaded, particularly in the winter. Learning how to get into a raft, then crank the "Gibson Girl" emergency radio, often meant the difference between life and death. *USAF*

sions on our airplane, and we got to know him pretty well. We admired him more than anybody else on the crew because here he couldn't shoot back at all, and he was running around the airplane, sticking his camera out, taking pictures! All of the footage didn't come from what he did. He gave out over two hundred 16mm cameras to the various groups, saying, "Now, if you get a chance, when you're not shooting your guns or whatever you're supposed to be doing, if you get a chance, take some film." And they did, resulting in this documentary. Then he gave the cameras to each one that took shots for him. He was a great guy. . . . I was really very fond of William Wyler. They gave him the air medal for those five missions.

I visited his home in Hollywood after the war. In his trophy room he had his Oscars all around, but right in the middle he had that air medal. He was more proud of that than he was of all his Oscars. And we were proud of him and the job he did. It was an unusual documentary done for the time because it was done in color. Most photography in World War II, in the early stages particularly, was done in black and white. This made it even more important. On some things in the film (not the shots in combat, not the scenes on the ground, but shots of the high command strategic planning of a particular mission—our twenty-fifth mission) they lied a little bit, I'm sure because they were pretty sure the Germans would get a copy of *Memphis Belle*. They wanted to make them think that we had all those airplanes on that drawing board up there— which we didn't, by any means, at that time. Of course we did later on, and the job done

after I left was even more fantastic. We were just the neophytes and the beginners. We did our part. . . . but we were glad to get back home.

John Ramsey
B-17 navigator, 493rd Bomb Group

In January 1945, members of our crew were sent to rest homes for a week, the four officers going to Eynsham Hall near Oxford. On Sunday the Yanks at the hall were transported to various places of worship, and the party I joined went to a small Methodist church in the town of Witney. We were ushered to seats on the left side of the sanctuary as one faced the chancel. There was a balcony along the full length of the opposite side, and in the end closest to the chancel was a group of children who had remained after Sunday school for the church service. The text of the sermon was introduced by the pastor's listing several leave-taking expressions, including "Adios," "Au revoir," the British expression of the day "God bless," and what he thought was the predominant American expression, "So long." He then asked the children in the balcony which expression they thought was the nicest and most meaningful. Obviously he expected their reply to be "God bless," which would lead him nicely into his sermon. Those kids looked down at the dozen or so Yanks in their proper dress uniforms and shouted as one, "So long." Whether it was the novelty of having Yanks in the congregation or just that natural rapport that seemed to exist between the US servicemen and the British kids didn't matter, but those kids really made the day for some homesick young

Nose art took on almost every imaginable form, as this 446th Bomb Group B-24 at Bungay demonstrates. *Albert R. Krassman*

Lieutenant A. J. Wood sits in the cockpit of his B-26 Marauder at Stanstead in mid-1944. The 344th Bomb Group had an outstanding nose artist who seemed to have no trouble painting just about anything on metal. *Jack K. Havener*

Yanks. We almost stood up and saluted our young friends. Needless to say, it took some adroit maneuvering on the part of the pastor to get back on track with his sermon.

Ben Smith
B-17 radio operator, 303rd Bomb Group

We didn't fly all the time. We would fly a mission, lick our wounds for a few days, then fly again. The weather was our worst enemy or friend, depending on how one looked at it. It kept us grounded a lot. This didn't bother anybody but a few brave souls. I was always glad to see the mission scrubbed because of bad weather. It meant I had another day to live.

When not flying, at four o'clock each afternoon we would go to the Red Cross for tea

October 1944. An absolutely stunning example of the 344th Bomb Group artist's ability to transfer the July 1943 Alberto Vargas *Esquire* gatefold to a Marauder. The aircraft was named *Valkyrie*, and here it waits to go on the next mission from the group's new base at Cormeilles-en-Vexin, France, which was coded Station A-59 by the Ninth Air Force. *Jack K. Havener*

The honcho nose artist in the 487th Bomb Group at Lavenham was Sergeant Duane Bryers. *Tondelayo* is an excellent example of his skill with paint. *Mark Brown/USAFA*

and crumpets, a rather tame repast for the aerial gunners. I grew quite fond of tea. It gave one a nice little pick-up. I thought tea a very civilized custom; in fact, we tended to ape a lot of the things the British did. They were not to be deterred from their tea. I am told British soldiers would make tea while they were being shelled. I was once in a barber's chair in Northampton when the town clock struck tea time. The barber left me sitting there in the chair with a partial hair cut as he went out for tea. Of course, he begged my pardon first.

When one of the 446th Bomb Group's nose artists had finished this beautiful girl, he began to paint the name *Black Magic* behind her. But he misjudged and ended up with only enough room for *Black M.* That didn't make much sense, so later he painted it out with fresh olive drab paint that is clearly visible on the original faded paint. *Albert R. Krassman*

Classy Chassy was a well-used name for wartime aircraft, certainly put to good use on this 446th Bomb Group Liberator out of Bungay. *Albert R. Krassman*

At times, names were bad omens. *Lassie Come Home* didn't make it back on 4 November 1944, and it was not only the single loss from the 446th Bomb Group but the only loss from the entire strike force. *Albert R. Krassman*

CHAPTER 4

Mission

Fritz Nowosad

group engineering officer, 384th Bomb Group

Typically I would be told at about 10:00 P.M. that I had to put up airplanes for a maximum effort mission. Work was taking place on the aircraft continually. . . . there was no eight-hour day. The group engineering officer would come around and say, "How many airplanes have you got serviceable?" I might say the best I could give was eight. Then he would go around the other squadrons and if everybody else had only eight, there would be only thirty-two of the needed fifty for the raid. So, he would come around again and say, "I need more." I would survey my boards and see which aircraft could be made ready if I concentrated men on these, then come back with, "Perhaps I can give you twelve." He would go around again, maybe get forty-six, then return around midnight or one o'clock in the morning saying, "You've got to give me thirteen airplanes." That's when the trouble began. "I can't give you thirteen airplanes. . . . I went

overboard giving you twelve." No use. "Look, I need thirteen to meet the requirement, and that's the end of it."

We would start to pull bits off other aircraft to make up the one serviceable one. My speech to the crew chief would go something like, "I don't care what you do, but I want that airplane working." How they did it sometimes, I don't know, but when I came back they would be replacing the cowlings, the engine would be fixed, and the crew chief would say, "Captain, it's ready to go." Borrowing, stealing, scrounging—somehow the airplane would always be made ready. GI ingenuity was unbelievable. They could put a B-17 together out of pieces, spray a serial number on it, and you would never know how it got there.

Pecos Reeves

B-17 ground crewman, 100th Bomb Group

It is very hard to say how we ground crew felt when our plane failed to return from a mission. We were never given any in-

A pair of 322nd Squadron, 91st Bomb Group B-17Fs climb to join the formation on the way to Germany in mid-1943. In spite of prewar faith in the ability of bomber formations to protect themselves from fighter attack, the opposite proved to be the case. Statistically the most dangerous place to be in combat that year, whether on the ground or in the air, and regardless of theater, was inside a bomber over Germany. *USAF*

B-17Fs of the 401st Squadron, 91st Bomb Group, low over England in early 1943. Based at Bassingbourn, the 91st was one of the pioneer Eighth Air Force heavy bomb groups, the first to attack a target in the Ruhr-Hamm area on 4 March 1943. Without extensive fighter escort through that year, the going was rough indeed. *USAF*

formation as to what might have happened. We would just stand around until dark, and, when there seemed like there was no hope, we would go help some other crew or go to the barracks. The next morning we would go to the flight line, hoping it would be sitting on the hardstand, but we knew better. You could count on it that you would be getting another aircraft in just a little while. If it was a new one, we would start stripping it, test fly it, and wonder how the new crew would accept us.

We knew that when the crew got in that machine in the morning, the chances of us never seeing them again were very real and likely. I just don't know how those guys did it. I never heard a whimper or a cry, and I only heard of one man in the 100th who refused to go. I guess there were more; I don't know. Our world and war was on that flight line. We never saw our officers or superiors unless they needed something. The aircraft was ours and ours alone until the flight crews came out and taxied out in it. We pulled all the pre-flights and post-flights on it. I never saw an air crew pre-flight one. They took our word for it: no questions asked, no problems.

Hubert Cripe
B-24 pilot, 453rd Bomb Group

Holding brakes to twenty-five inches mercury, brakes off, and the agonizing, slow roll of takeoff. Sweat, baby, sweat. Wide open throttles and 4,800 horses in the Pratt & Whitneys bellowed their song. Cool Hand Luke, the engineer, calmly called airspeed: sixty, sixty-five, seventy, eighty, ninety, ninety-five, one hundred. Holy Smokey, I can already see the end of the runway! Come on, baby: one-ten, one-twelve, one-fifteen, one-eighteen, one-twenty. Keep that nose down and get all that speed you can. At a hundred and twenty miles per hour I eased back pressure on the wheel, the heavy plane lightened, and we were airborne. Some terrific load—we can scarcely climb. "Gear up!" I screamed. "Gear up," came Russ's assuring answer, and the big gear swung outward and upward into the nacelles. Russ reset the manifold pressure and rpm, then milked up the flaps. At a hundred and fifty miles per hour we started climbing.

Robert Keir
B-17 tail gunner, 401st Bomb Group

We were the third ship to take off. We had just become airborne when the Fort

nosed up and the left wing dropped. We seemed to be going around in a big curve, and my first reaction was that our pilot was pulling a fancy maneuver. I got down on my left knee to look out the side window of the radio room in time to see the left wing throwing up dirt and sparks. Didn't have to be told we were in trouble, and, expecting a crash, I turned to brace against the radio room door. As I did, it swung open, and at first I thought someone was coming through. I held it and looked into the bomb bay, but there was nothing to see except those twelve 500-pounders. I shut the door and braced

myself against it and realized the pilot had got us off the ground. The engines were groaning, and I knew things were still very wrong. I glimpsed some guys standing by a hangar and wondered why I couldn't be there at this moment.

The plane struck the ground again, then cleared, but it was plain we weren't going to make it. I gripped the beading around the edge of the open radio room gun hatch and thought of trying to jump out, but things were going past too fast. Then we hit the ground hard, tail first, and I found myself looking out where the tail had been. Pieces

Bag of Bolts, **a 450th Squadron, 322nd Bomb Group B-26B, low over the Essex countryside, September 1943. The 322nd flew the first Marauder missions in the European Theater of Operations, paving the way through painful experience for a record that gave the B-26 the lowest loss rate of any Army Air Forces type in the war.** *Roland B. Scott*

Though not as well known as their Army counterparts, the US Navy flew the antisubmarine version of the B-24, the PB4Y. This PB4Y-1 out of England is hunting subs in the Bay of Biscay, 1944. In the face of strong enemy fighter resistance, Navy crews did a creditable job of sinking German U-boats. *National Archives via Stan Piet*

of fuselage were flying off and bulkheads were moving around and the ball turret was crushed up inside. The wreck was slowing, but I kept thinking about those bombs just the other side of that plywood door. A final big lurch and we came to a stop. I could see the reflection of flames on the aluminum skin.

I heard Musser say, "Let's get the hell out of here," as he jumped up and stepped over Cohen, who was lying by the ball turret. I walked over him too and out the fuselage side entrance. Cohen followed, and we all went around to the front of the wing and saw that the plane had hit a barn. The pilot had clambered out. He had blood running down his face. I was going back to get the bombardier and navigator, but the pilot said

they were dead and we should get clear before the bomb load went up. We ran down the field towards the village. A man stuck his head out of the first house and said, "Did you hear a bang?" I said, "You gonna hear another one in a minute." We told him to get his family out and down the road. There was a straw stack in the field near the road, and we all got behind that.

People were now coming down the road like a load of refugees. I took a look back at the plane and saw it was burning fiercely. There was nothing the crash wagon could do but let it burn and get people away from neighboring houses. Then, about fifteen minutes later, there was one hell of a boom and for a moment the clouds in the sky turned red. Pieces started to fall, the heavy

bits first and then the lighter pieces, which seemed to take a few minutes to come down. Many of the houses in the village were wrecked by the blast, but no one was seriously injured. The bombardier and navigator survived too, so all the crew escaped with their lives, if not without injury.

John Gabay

B-17 tail gunner, 94th Bomb Group

Wilhelmshaven, Germany, 3 February 1944 (ship number 846). Target: sub pens. It seems we made this raid the hard way, under very bad weather conditions. We had complete ten tenths cloud cover up to 20,000 feet. We had fairly good escort for a while. We ran into heavy but not so accurate flak as we crossed the enemy coast. On the bomb run, the bomb bay doors stuck, so Mike had to crank them down—in time to drop on target. Flak was heavy, but over on our left. We were to come out by way of the North Sea. A sleet storm reached our altitude, and we couldn't see to stay in formation, so we got orders that everyone was on their own. Ice was forming on our wings as we let down through the storm.

The last thing I saw before the weather enveloped us was a Fort running into the tail of another . . . chewed it up so bad the gunner fell out over the North Sea. I couldn't see anything else as the weather closed in around us. We dove at great speed trying to get to warmer air. The ice soon broke away from the wings, and we didn't hit anything—so far so good! We broke out through the clouds about 200 feet over the North Sea along the Frisian Islands. Now plenty of 20mm were bursting around the tail and left waist—couldn't see where it was coming

from. Then weather opened up and we saw soldiers running for their gun positions. We opened up on them—saw about twenty go down like rag dolls—and got out of there fast. Was a bumpy ride home. Found myself in midair several times.

Roy Kennett
B-24 radio operator, 392nd Bomb Group

Now, when we released the bombs, I was down on the catwalk. Bomb bay doors were open, and the bombs were gone. Then I had to say, "Bombs away, Sir!" Big deal, right? On the first mission I flew, I was a substitute radio operator; their guy had taken a hit, so I flew with this other crew. In fact, it was the first day we got to Wendling and the 392nd. Now their waist gunner was a big, tall, blonde guy, and it was his job to tell the pilot when the bomb bay was clear. He was a good guy, but he had a heck of a stutter. Well now, we're leaving the target, and he's down on the catwalk calling to the captain. We're all listening for him to say, "Bombs away,

Late 1944. A 385th Bomb Group B-17G climbs out from Great Ashfield and heads for Germany. *Clark B. Rollins, Jr.*

Wading through flak on the bomb run, as seen by a tail gunner in a 385th Bomb Group B-17 in late 1944. The twin smoke trails are from the target markers released by the lead aircraft. *Clark B. Rollins, Jr.*

Sir." So he says, "Ba-ba-ba-bob-ba-bob-bo . . . (Silence.) The goddamn things are gone, Sir!" That was a tough mission, but we all broke up over that one.

Ed Leighty
B-17 waist gunner, 447th Bomb Group

I shall never forget the briefing for that mission, the first daylight attack on Berlin. The intelligence officer was a big man; he looked as if he had lived a good life. He pulled back the curtain over the wall map, and there was the target marked out by a long wool string from England to Germany. "Men," he said pointing with his stick, "today you will bomb Berlin." I don't know about any men being there in the room, but I know there were a lot of frightened boys.

Ben Smith
B-17 radio operator, 303rd Bomb Group

After three missions, I was beginning to swagger a bit. I went out of my way to paint lurid pictures of aerial combat to the green crews coming in as replacements. Really there was no need to exaggerate. The empty beds in the huts were silent witnesses to that fact. I suppose veteran warriors from time immemorial have sought to frighten their novice companions. But none was more vocal than I was in describing the maniacal fury of the German opposition. This bombastic euphoria was of short duration, however. It had been rumored in the squadron that we would be one of the lead crews after Captain Brinkley's crew finished their tour. This belief was reinforced when a bird

A 367th Squadron, 306th Bomb Group Fort climbs out from Thurliegh as it passes directly over Benson Airfield, Oxfordshire. *Ben Marcilonis via Roger Freeman*

The 490th Bomb Group heads into Germany, far from home. *Albert N. Delmonico*

colonel flew with us on one of our early missions, ostensibly to look us over. When we came off the target, it was my job to look in the bomb bay and see that all the bombs had cleared the racks. On this mission the flak was really coming up, so I hastily looked in the bomb bay, closed the door, and yelled, "Bomb bay clear." I had seen no bombs. When we got down from altitude and were out over the Channel, I started through the catwalk, and, to my horror, half the bombs were in the bomb bay and still fully armed. Since we were nearing the English coast, Chick and the colonel decided to land with the bombs. They were too costly to jettison. We flew back to the 303rd and landed safely. Chick made a perfect landing. Thank God

he did. I knew I was going to catch hell. For some reason the colonel did not chew me out, but I could see he was sore as hell. I had really blown it. We heard nothing more about "lead crews," and my crew members blamed me for the fact that we were passed over. I had endangered the whole crew needlessly, and I felt awful about it. I was completely deflated, a condition which became me more than my previous swaggering. When we were down, Chick looked at me and said, "For Chris's sakes, Smitty," but that's all he ever said.

Marauders of the 495th Squadron, 344th Bomb Group marshal at A-59, Cormeilles-en-Vexin, France, in October 1944 for takeoff against targets in the Cologne area as the Allied armies push toward Germany. *Jack K. Havener*

A well-worn 386th Bomb Group Marauder over occupied France, 1944. At this point, war paint wasn't much of an issue. If it stayed on, fine; if it didn't, so what. *John H. Meyers*

Roy Kennett
B-24 radio operator, 392nd Bomb Group

There could have been about 155 fighters in the area, but not all attacking our particular group. They were Focke-Wulf 190s. Now an Fw 190 looks a lot like our P-47s—it's got that oval configuration with a slight dihedral to the wings, and the Fw 190 looks just like it. We thought they were ours—until they started shooting at us. We had been escorted by P-38s, and they had just left us because their range wasn't long enough. The P-47s were supposed to pick us up. All I remember is that their wings sparkled. It looked like they had headlights, and they were turning them on and off on the leading edge of the wing.

All of a sudden, all hell broke loose. When we got hit, a fire broke out in the airplane, and it spread into the bomb bay. So I went down into the bomb bay and tried to get the fire out—it was around the bombs because we still had our bombs in the air-

craft. The bomb bay went open while I was on the catwalk. The fire was just tremendous by that time, and there was no chance of getting it out. It was all over everything. Gasoline was pouring down into the bomb bay and was feeding the fire, so I looked upwards toward the flight deck. . . . the copilot was standing there motioning for me to get out. I walked up out of the bomb bay into that well that goes into the command deck, grabbed my parachute, and snapped it on. I grabbed at Krushas's feet a couple of times and yanked on them. Then I turned around on the catwalk and rolled out of the bomb bay.

Krushas was in his turret when it got shot out and it was inoperable. He looked down and saw fire around his feet, so he crawled out of his turret and looked around for me. I was gone, so he said, "If it's no place for Kennett, then it's no place for me." He grabbed his chute, snapped it on, and jumped out too. He said, when he got out,

103

the pilot and copilot were both in their seats trying to fly the airplane. Now back in the waist, where Hatton was, Smitty had one waist gun and Hatton had the other waist gun. Rowlett was in the tail and Oliver Schmelzle was in the ball turret. I can't remember if the ball turret was hurt or not, but they got the turret up into the waist of the airplane and got Schmelzle out. And the airplane still hadn't gone down! The tail gunner got out of the tail section and came back into the waist. I don't know if it was three minutes, five minutes, or ten minutes, but it was more than just a few seconds.

So then all four were around the camera hatch. Smitty told me that Hymie Hatton

The 457th Bomb Group begins to pull contrails as it crosses into enemy airspace, late December 1944. No one liked to see these plumes of vapor coming from the exhaust of each engine; they virtually pointed German fighter pilots and flak gunners to their targets. *Leslie R. Peterson*

Pulling some maintenance at Mendlesham on the 34th Bomb Group's *Ole Timer*, a 391st Squadron ship, while there's a respite between missions. *Mark Brown/USAFA*

was down on his knee, right alongside the open camera hatch, motioning for Schmelzle and Rowlett to jump. Smitty was standing up right beside Hymie. Schmelzle and Rowlett were just standing there and wouldn't jump, so then Hatton jumped. Smitty went right down alongside the hatch and tried to get Rowlett to jump, but he just stood there. Just about that time, the ship snapped into a spin. It threw Smitty halfway out. He said to me, "The last thing I saw when I looked back was Schmelzle and Rowlett stuck to the bulkhead by centrifugal force." Then the slipstream tore him out.

Now, the sound of being pulled out into the slipstream—you'd almost have to hear

it, and a person telling you probably can't describe it either. The best way I can think of to describe what happens when you first jump out of an airplane is this: If you're traveling down the road in an automobile and you throw a piece of paper out the window, you notice how it flutters and turns and does all kinds of whirligigs, and then all of a sudden it just calms down and very gently floats down to ground. Well, the initial reaction to a jump is very much the same. When I rolled off that catwalk and into the slipstream, it just turned me every which way but loose for a few minutes. Then it sort of comes down to your normal falling speed—around 120 miles per hour. But you have no

Changing engine number two, 18th Squadron dispersal, 34th Bomb Group, Mendlesham, 1945.
Mark Brown/USAFA

sensation of falling, because you have no reference point. If you fall off a ladder, you can see the house go by. When you're five miles up in the air, you're not passing anything (although there were pieces of airplanes falling down all around you). It isn't noisy; you don't hear anything but the wind whistling next to your ears. I know when I first came back, I told my father I had glided for over four miles before I pulled the ripcord.

Jack Havener
B-26 pilot, 344th Bomb Group

Uncle Sam always wanted value for his dollar, and this certainly applied to the payloads of World War II bombers. A combat overload was more the rule than the exception, especially with the B-26s, which we regularly flew off at 40,000 pounds, gross, when the manufacturer's maximum recommendation was 37,000 pounds. Every bomber pilot's dread was the loss of an engine on or soon after takeoff. We B-26 men were almost conditioned into believing that if this happened a crash was inevitable. Confidence was maintained because you hoped it only happened to the other guy. This time it didn't—it happened to me!

On 12 September 1944 our group was briefed to bomb strong points at Foret de Haye near Nancy, France. I was flying *Terre Haute Tornado* with First Lieutenant William R. Hunter as my copilot. I had flown copilot for Hunter a few days previous in his regular lead ship, and now he was flying co for me in my regular one. On these extra missions, we normally carried our regular crew with the exception of the bombardier and the navigator. Lead bombardiers were zealously relegated to lead missions only, so this routine gave wing position bombardiers a chance for extra missions also. On this one we had one of the few remaining sergeant bombardiers on board, Phil Dolce. Likewise, since we were flying a wing position, we didn't need a navigator.

We had just taken off to the northeast and were about halfway through the first turn to join up with the balance of the flight on our left, when the right engine started sputtering and losing power. We were only at about 1,000 feet, and as we frantically clawed the pedestal controls, trying to get some life back into the engine, we realized we had a serious problem. Naturally we couldn't gain altitude, so we abandoned the attempt to join up with the flight and turned on the downwind leg of the traffic pattern, trying to maintain flying speed.

When it was obvious that the engine would not respond, I gave Hunter the order to feather the prop. By the time I had trimmed for single-engine operation we were still losing altitude, so I gave Sergeant John Skowski, our engineer-gunner, the signal to pull the emergency bomb salvo release. He always stood between the two pilot seats on takeoff to keep an eye on the instruments. He immediately reached up and pulled the release to dump the four 1,000-pounders we were carrying, turned around to watch the bomb bay doors open and snap shut after the salvo, and greatly relieved the tension in the cockpit when he yelled, "We got a haystack, Lieutenant!"

Hunter kept calling out airspeed as we continued on the downwind leg and called the tower, informing them of our situation and requesting permission to land immediately. In a very cool tone the tower operator came back, telling us he had a formation still taking off and could we please hold for a bit until all the ships were off? Hunter and I stared across at one another in disbelief, and he replied, "Hell no! We're on one engine just above stalling speed, and we're coming in if we have to land on the taxi strip!" His ruddy face turned even redder as he blasted this to the tower in a manner that only Willy could do.

We were so low (no more than 500 feet) that we couldn't see the field to our left but knew we were on a correct downwind heading and would begin our approach turn when we sighted the St. Giles church steeple at Great Hallingbury just off the southwest

Eighth Air Force Station 134, Eye, in the Suffolk countryside, home of the 490th Bomb Group. *Mark Brown/USAFA*

end of the runway a couple miles. Then pre-stall vibrations set in, and I told Hunter, "We can't make it. Let's land on the RAF fighter field just ahead of us." Before he could answer, the Royal Air Force field loomed ahead where tractors were pulling mowing machines across the center of the grass. How do you decide what to do in a situation such as this? Sacrifice two lives on the ground in hopes of saving six in the aircraft, possibly wiping out the aircraft in the process, or save the two on the ground and try for the good old Stanstead runway? The Royal Air Force field was Sawbridgeworth, by the way.

As if reading my thoughts, Hunter said, "We've got to make it! Just keep her from stalling and do a flat pylon turn around the steeple!" I agreed and began a gentle turn to the left with the steeple as my bearing point. Not wanting to lose any more altitude than necessary, I kept the turn very shallow and silently prayed a thanks to Mr. Ransom,

This 490th Bomb Group B-17G has just turned off the active runway at Eye after a mission and heads for its hardstand. *Mark Brown/USAFA*

my primary flight school instructor, for drilling into me the intricacies of a correct pylon turn. As a result, we rounded out the turn just southwest of the steeple and homed in on it to the northeast, looking for the end of the runway.

It's hard to believe, but my top-turret gunner, Sergeant J. E. Smith, who had dropped out of his turret and crawled into the navigator's chair when the engine quit, swore that I lifted the right wing to clear the St. Giles steeple. This done, I had Hunter drop the gear and flaps at the same time, and I chopped the throttle over the end of the runway, still managing to unwind the trim and keep her straight. With my preoccupation in winding out lateral trim, I didn't have time to adjust elevator trim on the round-out (flat as it was) and can thank Hunter for helping me pull back on the control column to keep us from going in too steeply.

Luckily, we had consumed enough time during our slow-flying transit of the traffic pattern to allow the rest of the formation to take off, and the runway was clear for the landing with the crash trucks, the ambulances, and the inevitable group commander's jeep racing down alongside us as we touched down and braked to a halt about halfway down the strip. The usual ground-kissing ritual was performed by the entire crew after we exited the aircraft, and my right arm was quivering from the crew shaking my hand. Sergeant Raymond C. Sanders, my radio gunner, says it was the only time he ever kissed a man when he planted a big one on my cheek. Under the circumstances, I didn't mind at all.

The colonel's jeep careened up, and he uncoiled that big frame and strode over to me. I thought, "Oh, oh, I'm going to catch hell now for aborting." Aborting with questionable cause was a no-no in the 344th, and

Bomb dump, 490th Bomb Group, Eye, England, late 1944. *Mark Brown/USAFA*

lately there had been some obvious incidents of "featheritis." My emergency was legitimate, and I was prepared to tell him so.

I saluted, and returning it, he asked, "What happened, son?" I related how she'd cut out after takeoff, and, despite all action by my copilot, she kept losing power so we had to salvo and shut her down. To my surprise, he stuck out that big paw and said, "Congratulations, Son. You did a magnificent job of bringing her in and saving the airplane and your crew!" I was almost too taken aback to murmur, "Thank you, Sir," as he shook my hand. I stood transfixed as he

turned on his heel, climbed back in the jeep, and motioned his driver to move out, yelling to us all to go over to the flight surgeon for a shot of whiskey as he peeled away.

Just at that time, Staff Sergeant Jerry Reed, our crew chief, and the technical sergeant line chief arrived and were looking at the suspect engine and giving me jaundiced glances, so I opted to go with the aircraft as it was being towed back to the hardstand to try to find out what had caused the loss of power. Back at the hardstand, as the line chief ran the engine up to full power time and again with no drop in manifold

A 490th Bomb Group Fort begins a turn off the active runway at Eye after the long trip home from Germany. Flying B-24s, then B-17s, the 490th was one of the few good-luck groups in the Eighth, with one of the lowest combat loss rates.
Mark Brown/USAFA

pressure or the faintest hint of a sputter, I had the uneasy feeling that he was thinking, "Well, another pilot with featheritis." The next time he ran her up there was a definite sputtering and loss of manifold pressure. This repeated itself on subsequent run-ups, and he admitted that there seemed to be fuel starvation.

Subsequent investigation revealed a perforated carburetor diaphragm, which prompted a maintenance directive to go out and all engines in the group were checked for this fault. I never did find out how many more were faulty, but I know that they found some on other aircraft and consequently all diaphragms were replaced. It was one of those quirks that doesn't show up on a ground check but only manifest themselves under full power load in flight. I was vindicated!

After a meal at the mess, Hunter and I and an intelligence officer took off in the Ox-

ford Airspeed to plot the location of the jettisoned bombs. Retracing our previous calamitous flight pattern, as best we could, we found that Skowski was right. We had completely demolished a large haystack in a farmer's field but had caused no other damage or injury. Of course, the bombs hadn't been armed, so the haystack had been clobbered by impact alone. The armament crew went out and retrieved the bombs, and our personnel officer made arrangements with the farmer to pay for the damage.

By the time we were ready to take off in the Oxford, I had recovered from the shock of the experience but had developed a bad case of the jitters, so had prevailed upon Hunter to fly the Oxford. Old steel-nerved Willy rose to the occasion, and as we were starting our left turn after takeoff, I slyly reached over and pulled the right throttle back just enough to create a noticeable loss of rpm, yelling, "Oh, no! Not again!" Hunter's startled look changed into a grin as he saw what I was doing, and we laughed like idiots, bleeding off plenty of pent up emotions.

Johnny Miller
B-17 waist gunner, 100th Bomb Group

The 6 March 1944 mission to Berlin was a slaughter for our group. Most of our planes didn't make it back. It was so quiet. The men spoke in low, almost inaudible tones, if they spoke at all. There were many that wandered off by themselves wanting to be alone in their grief. Others, their eyes moist, stood silently. And many drank more than usual

At the end of the war, the Eighth Air Force was tasked with dropping a different kind of ordnance—food—on Holland. The Dutch were starving, and the quickest way to meet the need, until ground links could be set up, was to air-drop the food. This 34th Bomb Group B-17G, northwest of Amsterdam, is on the way back from Utrecht in May 1945. *Mark Brown/USAFA*

Our Baby, an 839th Squadron, 487th Bomb Group Fort with another of Alberto Vargas's famous *Esquire* girls on the nose, climbs out of Lavenham to drop napalm on the last German troop strongholds at Royan, near Bordeaux, 15 April 1945. *Mark Brown/USAFA*

111

The view from the tower at Snetterton Heath. Flying Fortresses of the 96th Bomb Group taxi out for takeoff, late 1944. This scene was duplicated across England, in everything but the aircraft markings, for three years, dozens of times each day. *Mark Brown/USAFA*

The 100th Bomb Group's airfield, Thorpe Abbots, mid-1944. *Lady Geraldine* has just been shut down in its hardstand after a mission, and the crew is trying to stretch the kinks out as cigarettes are lit up. A six-by-six truck and jeep stand ready to take them to interrogation. *Mark Brown/USAFA*

that evening. Lieutenant Colonel John Bennett, our squadron CO but now commanding officer of the group, grasping for some words to say, said the Eighth had lost less than ten percent. But his voice sounded strange, and his words trailed off.

I was living in the spare gunner's hut at the time, and for fifteen days following that raid on Berlin, I was alone in that hut! Everyone I knew was either killed or taken prisoner. *Less than two months* after joining my group, I became the oldest gunner in my outfit. I was seventeen years old.

A new engine has just been hung on the 100th Bomb Group's *Boss Lady* at Thorpe Abbots. The prop, in full feather position for positioning on the engine prop shaft splines, is getting its last bolts tightened before a ground check. *Mark Brown/USAFA*

CHAPTER 5

Combat

Ben Smith
radio operator, 303rd Bomb Group

I recall that I used to lie awake in bed dreading the time when I would have to lay it on the line or forever be lost in the infamy of disgrace (I learned later that I was not the only one). This was so real to me. Outwardly, I was lighthearted and jovial, well liked by my friends. They thought I was a pretty cool customer, but inside I was sick, sick, sick! My bravado was sort of a rallying point, though phony as a three-dollar bill. I wore a "hot pilot's" cap, smoked big black cigars, and drank boilermakers. The only one who wasn't fooled was me.

Richard Fitzhugh
B-17 pilot, 457th Bomb Group

Our bombardier crawled through the top turret one time on the way to pull the pins on the bombs (the engineer would have to step down and get out of there). And going through there, he caught some part of his flying equipment on the trigger that makes the turret go round and round. The harder

he pulled, the faster this thing went, just beating him to a pulp. The harder he tried to get out, the faster that thing went. Finally the engineer came to his rescue, and they got him disentangled from that thing. I thought we were going to lose a bombardier that day.

John Gabay
B-17 tail gunner, 94th Bomb Group

16 October 1943: Today was a sad one. Our radio man, Charley Gunn, went on his first raid with another crew and all hands failed to return. There was a cablegram waiting for him—his wife gave birth to a baby boy. He'll never know.

Roy Kennett
B-24 radio operator, 392nd Bomb Group

After the plane took off and we made formation, you had to maintain radio silence. So I didn't have anything to do. As soon as we got over enemy territory, that was it. All I did was sit there. Sometimes that's the scariest thing—to be just helpless. My job

A B-17 navigator at his station. I guess the Army Air Forces photographer didn't think to hide the still propeller visible through the window, but this is still an excellent look at how a navigator went to war in the Eighth Air Force. *USAF*

was to take over if someone else was hit; I would take over his position. Thank God I never had to do that—until the very last mission, and then it was over.

Al Keeler
B-17 copilot, 95th Bomb Group

We were returning from a bombing mission to Trzebinia, Poland, and were well within friendly territory, descending through 10,000 feet on our way to land at our "shuttle raid" base at Poltava in the heart of the Ukraine. Our aircraft, *Full House* (so named because of its serial number: 2977797), with the appropriate five-card display on our nose, was leading the high squadron. I was the copilot. As we de-

Almost home, 26 August 1944. After hitting Brest, the 388th Bomb Group lets down over the English countryside on the way in to Knettishall. *Mark Brown/USAFA*

Not until 1945 did the Eighth get some Army OA-10A Catalinas to supplement the Royal Air Force's air-sea rescue (ASR) aircraft. Unfortunately, red tape kept them from arriving earlier. Still, the 5th Emergency Rescue Squadron put them to good use, losing two, one to enemy fire. This Cat is paying a visit to the 4th Fighter Group at Debden. *F. M. "Pappy" Grove*

One of the most welcome sights of the war, if you were an airman down in the English Channel—a Royal Air Force rescue High Speed Launch at the dock ready to cast off. The Royal Navy was also a part of the ASR fleet with similar Rescue Motor Launches. These brave air force and navy sailors meant business, at times taking extreme risks to get to crews, even using the cannon on the bow if that's what it took. These fast PT-boat types, based at Harwich and Great Yarmouth, performed the majority of wartime rescues at sea. *F. M. "Pappy" Grove*

An 18th Squadron, 34th Bomb Group B-17G sits out an approaching storm while visiting Mt. Farm. *Robert Astrella*

parted 9,500 feet, I called over the interphone, "Copilot going off oxygen," meaning that I would remove my oxygen mask and change to a throat mike for the lower altitude.

Suddenly, a small oxygen explosion occurred under the base of the top turret gunner, Staff Sergeant Ray Rich. Immediately the cockpit filled with smoke. The pilot, First Lieutenant George Dancisin, who was still hooked to his oxygen tube and helmet headset, bolted out of his left seat, separating his oxygen hose, headset cord, and oxygen mike cord. Since this occurred as I was changing to my headset and throat mike, no other crew members had interphone contact with the cockpit. After Danny left his seat, I was

immediately flying the aircraft. The smoke became so dense I could hardly breathe. Fortunately, our B-17 had a small window vent panel on the front windscreen that could be opened. I grabbed for it and immediately the slipstream from the open panel helped clear the instrument panel so I could check our altitude. We were in a loose formation, so I peeled away from the group in a sharp right turn—no place for a burning aircraft that might explode and take some other aircraft down with it. I leveled the aircraft at a safe distance in line with the rest of the group.

The cockpit became even more drafty as Danny, who had climbed down into the nose, had told the navigator, First Lieutenant Frank Morrison, and the bombardier, First

Lieutenant Foster Sherwood, to bail out through the lower nose hatch. Why Danny did not bail out then I'll never know. Evidently, it suddenly dawned on him that he was the pilot and there were other crew members still in the aircraft! He came back up to the cockpit and said, "Rube [my nickname], we're bailing out!" I had reached for my chest pack to buckle it on while Danny was down in the nose. No chute! We always hung our chest packs on the back of each other's seat for easier access to grab them. Danny had taken my chute and climbed back down into the nose preparing for bailout. I reached in back of Danny's seat, and evidently in the melee, Danny's chute had fallen off its hook. Through the smoke, I

A 95th Bomb Group Fort just airborne at Horham, August 1944. *Albert J. Keeler*

A part of the 412th Squadron, 95th Bomb Group crew of *Full House* on top of their B-17G at Horham, summer 1944. (Left to right): right waist gunner Staff Sergeant Bob Rogers, ball turret gunner Staff Sergeant Leo Makelky, top turret gunner Staff Sergeant Ray Rich, radio operator Technical Sergeant Alyre "Joe" Comeau, and tail gunner Staff Sergeant Larry Stevens. *Albert J. Keeler*

First Lieutenant Albert Keeler was copilot on the 412th Bomb Squadron's *Full House* from April to August 1944. Like most Army Air Forces pilots, he left peacetime pursuits (in this case studying to become a music teacher at Ithaca College, New York) to enter flight training. By the time he had completed thirty-five missions, flying had firmly taken hold, and Al made the Air Force a career, flying another combat tour in Korea in the process. *Albert J. Keeler*

reached down and felt a back harness moving—Rich! I yelled, "Hey, Rich, find me a chute!" We always carried spares in the lower cockpit area. He threw one up to me and, at about the same time, located a fire extinguisher. After a couple of squirts of the CO_2 bottle, the fire was out under the turret.

Just as the smoke was clearing, the door to the front of the bomb bay opened. It was Technical Sergeant Langford, the engineer, with a large fire extinguisher. He had been riding as waist gunner and had smelled smoke in the rear of the aircraft. He couldn't make interphone contact with the cockpit, so he had grabbed the big fire extinguisher and crawled between the bomb racks with *no chute* on, because he couldn't climb through the racks with it on and still carry

the extinguisher. What guts! With the fire out and cleared, I rejoined the formation and checked in with the lead, advising them that we were OK to continue back to Poltava with no emergency landing requirement. After the smoke cleared from the turret area, the base of Rich's turret was red hot! Some of the flames had blasted against the fuel transfer valves and burned some of the paint off the nameplate! Rich's chute, which he had buckled on during the incident, had one end of its packing burned out! Rich had minor burns on his hands.

I put Rich in the left seat, and we continued on back to land at Poltava. Danny came back up to the cockpit and stood between our seats, stone silent and ashen white. When we got on the ground, we later

found out that Morrison and Sherwood had been located by the Russians and would be returned to Poltava. Danny and I discussed the whole incident. I was pissed off, because so many of us were deserted in a burning aircraft, and I wanted to recommend Rich for an award, since he got the fire out, saving the rest of us. We were near the end of our combat tour. This had been our thirty-second mission. With two more missions back to England, via Foggia, and probably "milk runs" (they were!), we decided to forget the whole deal. There might have been a lot of questions asked, and Danny, who had been a fine pilot, might have had a rough time of it if the facts had come out.

Frank Morrison
B-17 navigator, 95th Bomb Group

I think most crews in the 95th could be described as crews of "extreme camaraderie." I had to make up three missions as the result of being hospitalized and, again, three more as a result of a parachute jump. I have seen a blow-up color photo of the crew sitting by the runway at Horham, waiting for my make-up plane to return. On my thirty-fourth mission, the balance of the crew already having flown thirty-five, we all received a good scare. I guess I would have to say that 26 August 1944 was a day when it could have gone either way.

We took a series of flak hits over the target at 26,000 feet, and with two engines out and a broken oxygen line, we could not take evasive action to escape the extremely heavy ground fire. We began to gradually lose altitude, and we called for a fighter escort. Almost at once those beautiful P-51s

95th Bomb Group crew of *Full House* outside their Nissen hut briefing room at Horham, summer 1944. Back row: pilot First Lieutenant George Dancisin, navigator First Lieutenant Frank Morrison, right waist gunner Staff Sergeant Bob Rogers, bombardier First Lieutenant Foster Sherwood, and tail gunner Staff Sergeant Larry Stevens. Front row: copilot First Lieutenant Al Keeler, radio operator Technical Sergeant Alyre "Joe" Comeau, top turret gunner Staff Sergeant Ray Rich, and ball turret gunner Staff Sergeant Leo Makelky. *Albert J. Keeler*

appeared and stayed right on our wing tips as we limped for the coast. The Me 109s just loved to get a wounded B-17 alone, but they surely didn't want to tangle with a couple of P-51s. As we reached the Channel, we were down to near 1,000 feet, and the pilot gave the order to jettison all expendable cargo. That seemed to be just enough to let us land at the first fighter base on the English shore. My estimation of B-17 pilots, which was already good, went up 1,000 percent. If they were good enough to be in the 95th, they were good enough for me.

Meanwhile, back at Horham, my crew was watching the squadron return as usual, and all the planes were accounted for except one, and that was the one I was flying with that day. They hurried over to question some of the other crews and were told of us losing altitude with two feathered props and being unable to keep up with the formation. When they went back to the Quonset, I guess it was a pretty sad evening. At last we were furnished a ride from the fighter base back to Horham. When I walked into the Quonset, there were some damp eyes among these so-called "tough" sergeants. I will say that the "welcome" was followed by one helluva party. And then I received the icing on the cake. The following day I was notified by Colonel Carl Truesdell that I might just be trusting my luck a bit too far, and if I so desired, I could go home with the rest of the crew, even though I had only flown thirty-four missions, and they had flown thirty-five. I have never met Colonel Truesdell

The 344th Bomb Group climbing out of Stanstead, England, for a support mission, June 1944. *Jack K. Havener*

The 7th Bomb Squadron's *Flying Dutchmen* gets some much needed post-mission maintenance at Mendlesham, home of the 34th Bomb Group. *Mark Brown/USAFA*

since that day, but I've always had a soft spot in my heart for him. Again that night, we had one of those parties to remember.

Richard Fitzhugh
B-17 pilot, 457th Bomb Group

On the missions we didn't have any food, so they'd give us a big square of chocolate for the crew. One great, big solid piece of chocolate. On the way back, the engineer would break this up and pass it out for a little nourishment. Sometimes it would get so cold—it might be seventy below up there—

that he would take the fire ax and lay this chocolate down on the sheet metal floor of the B-17 and hammer on it. The first time I heard him doing that, I thought he was firing the guns up there. He'd bang on that thing and break it up, but then it was so cold you couldn't hardly put it in your mouth.

John Gabay
B-17 tail gunner, 94th Bomb Group

History of ship number 846, named *Lucky 13* by ground crew: Lawrence Kersey, Don MacConnell, Leroy Kriest. First B-17G

With one B-24 on the runway about to release brakes, the 493rd Bomb Group marshals for takeoff at Debach, June 1944.
Mark Brown/USAFA

125

Two 490th Bomb Group Forts are already on the runway at Eye with a third on short final, while the next squadron is on initial approach for the overhead break to landing. By this time in the winter of 1944–45, the Eighth Air Force had worked out an excellent recovery procedure with minimum spacing between landing bombers. An entire group could land in short order if everyone was sharp; and everyone usually was, since landing was considered the test of a pilot's ability. *Mark Brown/USAFA*

to be assigned to 331st Squadron on 28 October 1943. Twenty-fifth mission on 11 March 1944. Fiftieth mission 28 June 1944. First G to make fifty missions in 94th. Made "war weary" on 11 October 1944. Seventy-eight missions, 935 hours. Two large Ws painted on rudder. Will go to sub depot for major overhaul after 1,000 hours. Went on first and only shuttle mission to Africa after Regensburg raid. Fifteen engine changes, three oil coolers, two superchargers, one wing tip, one outer wing panel, two inner gas tanks, one rudder, one elevator, one right stabilizer, one rudder control cable, one tail wheel, seven tire changes, two de-icer boots, one patch on Plexiglas nose, hundreds of patches, one flat on landing, running off runway into mud. Spent all night getting it changed.

Bob Morgan
B-17 pilot, 91st Bomb Group

It was a great airplane for a number of reasons. The first is that it would take a lot of punishment—a lot of punishment. I can vouch for that, and I'm sure any other B-17 pilot that flew the airplane in combat can say the same thing. I flew B-29s in the Pacific after I left the European theater, and people have asked me to compare the '29 and the '17. The '29 would never have lasted in Europe, and there was a thought to take it over there at one time. It could never have taken the punishment the '17 did. We lost more B-29s from mechanical failure than we did from the Japanese. If it had been in Europe, it would have been a dead dog. It was a great airplane, don't get me wrong, but the '29 was built for a particular purpose: long-

range, Saipan and Guam to Japan. It could carry a big load, but it was not the airplane that could take the punishment from the accurate German antiaircraft and the German fighters.

I get a little flak once in a while from B-24 pilots, and I have friends who flew the B-24. The prettiest sight in combat when we went over France and Germany was to see a B-24 group, 'cause if we saw a B-24 group, we knew the German fighters would not pick on us so badly that day. That's not a nice thing to say, but it is, honestly, truthful.

Besides the B-17, there was one other factor—the Norden bomb sight. A lot of people overlook that fact. The British didn't have it; no one else had it but us, and it was accurate. I'll always remember one mission in January of 1943. We were the lead ship going over Lorient to bomb some submarine pens from 26,000 feet. The photographs showed that the main impact point of the first bomb was ten feet from the center of the target the bombardier was supposed to hit. That is pretty accurate. They awarded him an air medal for that particular raid.

Bob DeGroat
B-24 pilot, 459th Bomb Group

On one mission, while still over enemy territory, a P-51 slid in and flew formation off my left wing. A voice on the radio casually asked, "Big Brother, mind if I join you?" His engine was running rough and in this situation our guns would be able to cover him. It was a chance for us to protect him for

Some 487th Bomb Group B-17Gs taxiing back in at Lavenham after the 15 April 1945 mission to Royan, France. *Mark Brown/USAFA*

The 446th Bomb Group begins to come alive as the sun rises at Bungay, winter 1944–45. *Albert R. Krassman*

a change. He left us at the head of the Adriatic.

Bud Guillot
B-24 waist gunner, 392nd Bomb Group

The first time we saw a P-51 escort, we almost shot them down. We were on a mission to a six-engine bomber school, and it was over the other side of Munich—a long haul for us. Most of our fighters couldn't go that far, so we thought they were Me 109s. Instead of coming up beside us and slowly moving in, they came in nose first from six o'clock. It was a new aircraft, and we were new, so we didn't recognize them. In the blink of an eye we would have opened up on them. Lark Morgan, our tail gunner, called

up to Kamy and said, "Hey, there's four ships back here—I can't identify them." Kamy said, "Well, watch them and if they come in too close, shoot the hell out of them!" Lark looked back. "They're getting too damn close!" So Kamy said, "Go get 'em." Just then they rocked their wings up to identify themselves. I think they were new at their jobs too, otherwise they wouldn't have gotten that close to a bomber's tail!

Louis Kandl
B-17 pilot, 96th Bomb Group

On all our raids of not too great a length, P-47s give us cover. We could kiss every one of them; they're that good. Many a Fortress crew owes their lives to these buzz boys. They stick to you like glue when you're crippled.

George Meshko
B-17 waist gunner, 96th Bomb Group

Returning over our base, we buzzed the field and shot off two boxes of flares—about 200 rounds—to celebrate the completion of our combat tour. Our tail gunner was firing a Very pistol out the waist window and lobbed one right into the control tower. We all got a big kick watching the "brass" scramble. Our pilot, Lieutenant Thompson,

A 490th Bomb Group B-17 revs up for takeoff, as other Forts taxi up to the active runway at Eye, winter 1944–45. *Arnold N. Delmonico*

129

Invasion stripes never did wear very well, but no one really cared by the time the D-day invasion was history, as this 596th Squadron, 397th Bomb Group B-26B, *Dee Feater*, reveals while flying over the English landscape during late 1944. *Charles E. Brown/Royal Air Force Museum*

put on a real show for us—swabbing the field back and forth. What happy warriors we were in the B-17 that afternoon. We landed after nine hours aloft. I thought for sure we would never see England again since I had never expected to get back.

There at our hardstand to congratulate us on our tour completion were all our buddies, ground crew, and even the brass. As we came tumbling out of our ship, we were greeted with laughter, tears, hugs, back slapping . . . silent prayers.

In the wee hours of the morning, our gallant crew crawled in loose formation, leaving strange contrails across some muddy plowed fields from the combat club to our Nissen hut. Our tour completed, the only thing left was the hangover.

John Gabay
B-17 tail gunner, 94th Bomb Group

Cazuax, France, 27 March 1944 (ship number 540). Target: airdrome. Can't believe this is the last mission. Made it back OK. Had a celebration in the barracks. I was the first to finish from the barracks—fifty-two didn't make it.

Very short final, full flaps, coming back on the power. The B-24J *Betta Duck*, 7th Squadron, 34th Bomb Group, about to touch down. Wrinkled skin was a standard feature on Liberators, even new ones, but it never seemed to bother anyone. *Arnold N. Delmonico*

The 34th Bomb Group on the way back across the North Sea from a food drop mission to Utrecht, Holland, early May 1945. *Mark Brown/USAFA*

Ready to leave on a May 1945 food drop mission with the 385th Bomb Group, 3rd Air Division, headquarters photo officer Captain Mark Brown is dressed in regulation Army Air Forces flying gear—except for the Royal Air Force Type C helmet, which was much prized among American flyers. Thanks to this man, one of the finest collections of Eighth Air Force Kodachrome slides has been preserved for future generations. A look through the credits on these pages is ample testimony to his talent with a camera. *Mark Brown/USAFA*

Ready to drop food on Utrecht, Holland, in the first days of May 1945, the 385th Bomb Group has bomb bay doors open, wheels down, and partial flaps to get the bombers as slow as possible. Though this appeared to be safe enough, the slow speeds were very dangerous, particularly when flying in formation and making steep turns. Some of the Forts stalled out, and men were killed in this "biscuit bombing" campaign. *Mark Brown/USAFA*

Early May 1945. A 7th Squadron, 34th Bomb Group Fort leaves the Dutch coast on the way back to England from a food drop to Utrecht. *Mark Brown/USAFA*

CHAPTER 6

Fighters and Flak

Bob Kennedy
B-17 tail gunner, 303rd Bomb Group

It was a really nice day, as weather went for Germany. I sat back, enjoyed the view, and tried to acclimate myself to my new surroundings, not the least of which were the optical gun sight—my very first time in the tail with the same. Things up to, and including, the Initial Point run during which I had buried myself in the flak suit, naturally sitting on the apron to help later-life sexual adventures. Flak seemed neither heavy nor accurate. Off the run I started stowing things away while glancing rearward to see how the following group was doing. There was no following group—period! We'd heard no alarming "bandits in the area" call, which came when some group nearby was getting clobbered. I was still relaxed, looking rearward, when I picked up what looked like a dozen or so flashes pretty far back, like little flashbulbs going off. The only problem was I didn't know what it was! Later, after many conversations, we decided that I'd seen the Jerry fighters in the center of the wide,

sweeping left turn they made, when the sun glanced off their canopies.

Suddenly, all hell broke loose! A '17 to our rear began belching flames from number two engine and started peeling off. All this time there was *no* radio warning of attack. I stared in amazement as what looked like a hundred blurry shapes came in, all (in my mind) aiming directly at us. I was trying to get my helmet on when little firecrackers began breaking around the tail and the blurry shapes turned into fighters with wings and cowlings flickering with little lights. I tried to get my guns unlimbered; then some reflex action, probably terror, made me yell to the pilot, "Curley, the whole damn Luftwaffe is out here—*pull her up!*" What happened then took me and the waist gunner completely out of the action, but very probably saved our lives!

Neither I nor any of the crew had ever been on a '17 being yanked up and down—twice. Imagine the most vicious roller coaster ride possible, take off the restraints, load a bunch of goods around you, and you're in a

The 7th Photo Group's *Miss Nashville* was the only B-25 to serve in combat with either the Eighth or Ninth Air Force. Though originally sent to England in March 1943 to begin forming a Mitchell combat group, the bomber ended up doing communications work until it lost its original olive drab camouflage. According to Ed Hoffman of the 381st Air Service Squadron, crew chief Staff Sergeant Hicks asked for permission to strip and polish her. It was given, so he and his crew did the job; then a Varga Girl was painted on each side with the name. When Eighth Air Force commander Jimmy Doolittle—who had led the famous 1942 bombing raid on Tokyo in a B-25— *continued on next page* visited Mt. Farm, he couldn't resist flying the Mitchell for an hour. Later the plane was painted overall gloss black. White invasion stripes were added on the night of June 5, 1944, and the B-25 carried stripes below the wings and fuselage for the rest of its career. In August 1944 it flew thirteen night photo missions over V-weapons sites on the Channel coast. It was then relegated to carrying photos to Twelfth Army Headquarters as that army advanced across France. On 26 October 1944 it was heading for Hamm, a small forward field near Luxembourg City, where it dropped off its intelligence cargo. After takeoff for Mt. Farm, the B-25 was fired on and hit near Trier. Pilot Lieutenant Bob Kraft began looking for a field. Upon approaching Chalons-sur-Marne, France, the bomber burst into flame, but he got it down. The aircraft skidded off and into a tree, killing Kraft and the engineer, Sergeant Hicks. The copilot, Lieutenant Madden, was thrown clear, though he was badly burned. *Robert Astrella*

loose but confined space. That's it! I was smashed up and almost through the roof. Everything loose—flak suit, escape bag, shoes, helmet—all flew up and down with me and ended up in a heap flopping with me on the floor. Then before I could do much of anything, up, then down again! I fell over backwards, narrowly missing the seat horn with my crotch. This time, to give an idea of the sheer violence of the whiplashes, the ammunition on the right storage bin somehow jumped out and about five feet of heavy .50-caliber ammo added to the mess.

On my hands and knees, I tried to free my oxygen tube (caught in the ammo mess), get a glove back on (torn loose by the gun butts), and get the flak suit off me, along with the ammo, all at the same time. I glanced for a second out the right window and saw the crew coming out the waist of the nearest '17 off our left horizontal stabilizer. Still frantic to be able to move and breathe, in the next second I glanced up again and there sat—and I mean *sat*—an Fw 190 right off our left stabilizer, so close I could have wing-walked over to him. He must have just finished firing, because a yellow-white cloud of smoke came back from somewhere front like.

I think terror just took control because I can remember crawling over to the little exit door and putting on my chute (still in one piece) and just sitting, gasping oxygen, and praying to all gods I could think of, hoping I didn't miss any. Nothing, but nothing, happened. The plane still flew. I looked past the tail wheel housing and saw the waist gunner still alive and trying to get to his feet. Turned out he was pretty banged up during

the roller coaster ride. Getting a semblance of courage back, I tried to get the mess straightened out and my guns at least operative. Did some and finally mustered enough guts to look rearward and see how many Germans were still mad at our dear little tiger-tailed '17.

Nothing—pure, unadulterated, empty sky. I searched for our trailing squadron '17s. All gone. Pretty far below I could see one "falling leafing" all over the place. That was it! This time I really concentrated on finding the trailing group. Nothing—no group. Whatever segment of the Eighth this was—Wing, Division, or the whole Eighth—I had to face one fact: We were the last plane in the last formation. A *real* tail-end Charlie! About this time, I became aware that my radio wasn't working, got that straightened up, and called up front. Turned out they'd given up on me, and the waist hadn't heard anything since the famous "Pull her up." I told the pilot the situation, but he didn't believe that the rest of the squadron was gone. He did eventually.

The rest of the mission was routine except right after the onslaught when I was seeking to find *anything* in back of us. The call came in: "Fighters, twelve o'clock level coming in fast." Before I could get to my guns again, three or four P-51s flashed past to my left, really going all out. The pilot called that we were getting fighter cover front and rear and, this time, not German. I asked him if there was anything up front of us as there wasn't a *damn* thing in back of us. He assured me that we and the lead plane were closing up on another squadron

By mid-summer 1944, the early G-model Fortresses were beginning to show some serious wear, clearly evident on this 750th Squadron, 457th Bomb Group '17 from Glatton. *Robert Astrella*

(probably the 359th). But the sky sure was empty—all the way back.

I remember the pilot being chewed out for not using proper squadron landing procedures—and him telling them there was no squadron. Also the copilot "browning out" (losing bowel control) when, as he said, an Me 109 was so close he could kiss the Jerry pilot.

I can't remember one damn thing after the landing. *Nothing.* No battle damage inspections, no talking with the crew, and even nothing about the debriefing. Crazy, impossible, but true—a complete blank.

One thing sure about the mission. The Luftwaffe pilots were skilled operators. They didn't slash in but approached slowly and deliberately. They taught us a lesson for our few remaining missions—*alertness.* Never again did we relax—not ever!

Hans Iffland
Me 109 pilot, IV/JG 3

Normally we got up at about 6:00 A.M. and reported to the operations building at 6:30, where we had our breakfast. Officers and NCOs sat around chatting, some playing cards, others writing letters or reading books.

There were several rooms and offices in the operations building, as well as the main briefing room. There was a large gridded map on one wall of the waiting room, where the position of the bomber stream was marked when it began to come in. Next to the map was a large board with all of the pilots' names, their victory scores, which operations they had flown in, and when pilots had had to break off operations prematurely for any reason. So one could see at a glance which pilots had pressed on with their attacks, and which were liable to break away at the least sign of engine or other trouble. Obviously, if a man had engine trouble and returned early four times in a row, questions would be asked. The board also showed who was sick or wounded, who was on leave, etc.

While waiting, I would play cards or ping-pong.

This 554th Squadron, 386th Bomb Group B-26B from Great Dunnow, late summer 1944, has already seen a steady amount of action with the Ninth Air Force. The group hammered at a long list of strategic and tactical targets before being transferred to the Continent in October 1944. *Robert Astrella*

When the bombers were reported coming in, we had three states of readiness. First was 30 Minute Readiness: *"Achtung, Achtung, Achtung, Achtung, eine Durchsage: Ab sofort 30 Minuten Bereitschaft!"* This was a loose form of readiness, and meant only that the pilots were not allowed to leave the airfield. Normally martial music was played over the loudspeakers, and the announcements would interrupt this. Next readiness state was 15 Minute Readiness order as before, but *"15 Minuten Bereitschaft!"* Then came more music. On this order the pilots walked to the Staffel readiness rooms; next, they went to their aircraft dispersed around the airfield. Earlier in the day, each aircraft had been run up by the ground crewman, so each was ready for action, fully fueled up and armed. Each aircraft carried a drop tank under its belly. The engine had been warmed up first thing in the morning. At this stage, the pilots put on their life jackets and other flying clothing (though this was

often worn throughout the day).

Next stage was Cockpit Readiness: *"Achtung, Achtung, ab sofort, Sitzbereitschaft!"* The pilots walked over to their aircraft and climbed in, strapped on their parachutes, did up their seat harnesses, pulled on their helmets, and did up their radio connectors. Each Messerschmitt already had the large crank handle in place, sticking out the starboard side of the engine, ready for the engine to be started.

At Cockpit Readiness, the pilots could hear the fighter broadcasts via a telephone line plugged into each aircraft. Cockpit Readiness usually lasted no more than ten to fifteen minutes, though it could last for as much as an hour. For me, the minutes between being ordered to Cockpit Readiness and being given the order to take off were the most terrible of all. After the order came to get airborne, one was too busy to think about one's possible fate. But waiting to go, with nothing to do but think about what

might happen—that was the most terrible time of all. Would one still be alive that evening, or was this the beginning of one's last day? My own greatest fear was that I might be seriously wounded, with permanent injuries. Death was, of course, a fear, but that would have been the end. The thought of being left a cripple for the rest of one's life was, for me, the greatest fear of all.

At 11:37 came the order to scramble. A single green flare rose up from the operations building. The scramble takeoff was normal for a German fighter unit, with the aircraft of the three Staffeln and the Stab unit dispersed at four points equidistant around the airfield. On the order to scramble, two crewmen hopped onto the wing of the Messerschmitt and began turning the crank handle to get the heavy flywheel of the inertia starter revolving. They wound the crank faster and faster, then the pilot pulled a handle beside his right knee to clutch in the engine, which usually coughed a couple of times before starting with a throaty roar. After engine starting, the Stab took off first, straight out of their dispersal point. As they passed the center of the air-field, the tenth Staffel, situated ninety degrees to the left around the perimeter of the airfield, began its takeoff run. Then the eleventh, then the twelfth Staffeln. After takeoff, the Stab turned left, circling the airfield, and climbed away, collecting the tenth, eleventh, and twelfth Staffeln rapidly behind it. Once the Gruppe had assembled, the leader, Major Friedrich-Karl Mueller, swung it around to a southeasterly heading for Magdeburg.

When we were within about 800 meters of the bombers, we felt ourselves safe from the enemy fighters and had only the bombers' return fire to worry about. At such a range it was difficult to tell a Mustang from a Messerschmitt, and both would be shot at by the bombers' gunners. Our orders were to help the Destroyers punch through the screen of escorts, so that they could engage the bombers. I remember seeing the bomber formation like a swarm of insects in the distance.

It was terrible to have to attack the bombers, which opened fire at very long ranges (about 800 meters), while our Messerschmitts had only limited ammuni-

Ridden hard and put away wet, *Our Gal Sal* flew over 100 missions with the 100th Bomb Group out of Thorpe Abbots and finished the war to fly back home, only to be scrapped. Bob Shoens and his crew flew this Fortress to Berlin and back on 6 March 1944, the first all-out daylight mission to the German capital. *Robert Astrella*

139

An 18th Squadron, 34th Bomb Group B-24H from Mendlesham at rest with a trusty guard in front. It was not unusual for dogs to fly on missions, though this practice was strictly forbidden by Army Air Forces brass. Some dogs had their own oxygen masks and flying suits, and one was even rumored to have flown the low-level mission to Ploesti with the 44th Bomb Group. *Robert Astrella*

tion—we had to hold fire until within about 300 or 400 meters. This interception on 6 March 1944 was one of my first operational head-on attacks against an enemy bomber formation. The head-on attack was adopted because it was a more cost-effective way of engaging the bombers. When we attacked from the rear, there was a long period of overtaking when the enemy gunners were shooting at us, but we were not within range to fire at them. As a result, we sometimes lost more fighters than we shot down bombers. When we attacked from head-on, we were able to fire for only about one second, but the bombers were big, and we were relatively so small, that we were far more likely to hit them than they were likely to hit us. Our tactic was to attack by Staffeln in line abreast, so that the enemy bombers

could not concentrate their fire against any one of us.

During the firing run, everything happened very quickly. We were flying at about 450 kilometers per hour, and the bombers were flying at about 380 kilometers per hour, so closing speed was 800 to 900 kilometers per hour. After firing my short burst at one of the B-17s, I pulled up over it. I had attacked from slightly above, allowing a slight deflection angle and aiming at the nose. We knew that just a single hit with a 3cm explosive round would have devastating effects anywhere on the nose, but it was hardly possible to aim so accurately during the brief firing pass. I aimed at the nose, but saw the flashes of my rounds exploding against the Fortress's port wing root. And the whole time, we could see the tracer

rounds from the bombers flashing past us. I saw four or five rounds exploding around the wing root.

As I pulled up over the bomber, I dropped my left wing to see the result of my attack and to give the enemy gunners the smallest possible target at which to aim. I had also to pull up to get out of the way of the fire of the other Staffeln of the Gruppe coming in behind me. Of course, I did not want to ram the B-17. I saw the port wing of the B-17 slowly begin to fold up, and the bomber went down. Then I was out the back of the formation, and my main concern was to join up with other Messerschmitts of the Gruppe for the next attack.

On this day we knocked down thirteen bombers in return for only one of our fighters wrecked, and none of our pilots was killed or wounded. It seemed that we really were able to overcome the massive numerical superiority enjoyed by the enemy. We were astounded by our success, which gave us all new hope. We felt we really had grasped the problem of dealing with the great formations of bombers.

I tried to join up with machines from my Staffel, which carried white numbers. The eleventh Staffel had yellow numbers. If one was alone, one was highly vulnerable to attack from the Mustangs, and many of our fighters were lost that way. The Gruppe pulled around in a sweeping turn to the left of the formation, and then the fighters sped, flying a course parallel to and slightly above the bombers, overtaking them out of gun range as they moved into position for a second head-on attack. It was very important to deliver the second attack in line abreast with sufficient aircraft. If one or two attacked alone, the bombers would concentrate their fire on these, and that was extremely dangerous. Our orders were to continue attacking the bombers so long as we had ammunition and fuel. It was frowned upon if undamaged fighters returned with

This 332nd Squadron, 94th Bomb Group B-17G has had its chin and ball turrets removed to gain a little more performance—a clear sign of the air superiority the Eighth Air Force enjoyed in the last months of 1945. At this point in the war, the extra weight and drag was deemed more a hindrance than a help. *Robert Astrella*

141

The 93rd Bomb Group on the way to hit front line targets at Ahrweiler, Germany, 24 December 1944. The lead aircraft is a pathfinder, equipped with radar in place of the ball turret. *Glenn A. Tessmer*

fuel and ammunition remaining. Even if we had only ten rounds of cannon ammunition left, we were expected to deliver another attack against the bombers.

I came in for my second attack, but the target bomber made a slight turn, causing my rounds to miss. At the time of the first attack, the bombers had been flying in close formation. Now there were gaps in the formation, and the bombers were flying further apart so the pilot would have more room to maneuver. The B-17 snaked from side to side when I opened fire; it was enough to make the rounds miss during the brief firing pass. Then I was out of ammunition.

The most dangerous part of the engagement was getting through the screen of escorts. On this day we had done so without difficulty. Our orders were to engage the enemy fighters only when we had to. Otherwise we had to concentrate our attack on the bombers, which represented the greatest danger to our country. The only exception was when we were escorting the Destroyers.

Once one was out of ammunition, it was important to join up with other German fighters, because it was very dangerous if one was attacked by American escorts. If there were four or five of us together, the Americans would be more careful about attacking us. Also, being short of fuel, it was important to fix our position and decide where we were going to land.

On breaking away from the bombers, we went down in a rapid descent to about 200 meters to get well clear of the enemy fighters. At that altitude our camouflaged aircraft were very difficult to see from high above, while we could see the enemy machines silhouetted against the sky. A 200- to 300-meter altitude also gave us good R/T range, so we could contact our base. Sometimes we flew back even lower than that and climbed only when we wished to call our base to make sure it was safe for us to land there, since it might have come under enemy attack. When we arrived back over Salzwedel, we flew low over the airfield, and those pilots who claimed victories waggled their wings. I saw another aircraft in front of me doing it; then I did it. We knew we had been successful even before we landed. When we were overtaking the bombers for our second attack, we had seen some going down, others streaming fuel or smoke. One went down about 1,000 meters and then ex-

Cpls. Larry Roth and Wallace Merquardt move their radio-equipped control jeep out to the active runway at Mendlesham as a 34th Bomb Group Lib follows. Radio-equipped jeeps and mobile towers were an immense help in moving bombers and fighters to takeoff position in an orderly manner. *USAF*

143

Patches and *Sleepy Time Gal*, B-17Gs of the 532nd Squadron, 381st Bomb Group, climb out over England in late summer 1944. *USAF*

ploded. Another was on fire, and parachutes were coming from it. If there was a burning machine in the formation, the others would have to pull away from it in case it exploded. It made a vivid impression.

After landing and taxiing to the Staffel dispersal, the first to meet me was my mechanic. He had seen me rock my wings, and when I had shut down the engine and opened the hood, he stood by the trailing edge of the wing, clapped his hands above his head, shouted, *"Herr Leutnant, gratuliere!"* and offered me a cigarette. Obviously, if a pilot scored a kill, that counted for the mechanic also; it meant he had done a good job preparing the machine. No shortage of

cigarettes for the Luftwaffe; we were looked after very well as regards food and drink. I do not remember any problems when we operated in Germany, though there had been some difficulties in getting supplies through when we were in Italy.

When I reached the Gefechtsstand, our commander, Major Mueller, was already there receiving the reports from his pilots. I awaited my turn, then marched to the table. I clicked my heels, saluted, and proudly said, *"Melde gehorsamst. Vom Einsatz zurück. Eine Fortress abgeschossen!"* Then I explained how I had hit it and seen the wing fold up on the port side before it went down. *"Ach, das war Ihrer! Hab ich gesehen!"* ex-

A 91st Bomb Group crew chief, Master Sergeant Herbert H. Roberts, has just guided his Fort to a stop at Bassingbourn, late summer 1944. Though there was a defined chain of command up and down the enlisted and officer ranks, a crew chief made the final decision about the availability and condition of his airplane. In reality, it belonged to him, and though the aircraft commander could walk around, jiggle a few things, and kick the tires, if he wanted to know the exact status of the airplane, he asked the crew chief. *USAF*

claimed one of the other pilots. This was important, for without a witness, it was very difficult to get credit for a victory. Several other pilots said the same thing: The bomber had gone down in a spectacular manner, and several pilots remembered seeing it. *"Gratuliere!"* smiled Mueller. After me, other pilots reported kills. Each one was marked on the board beside the pilot's name, so soon it was clear we had had a very successful day.

Salzwedel was a permanent Luftwaffe airfield. Mueller announced, when the Gruppe was stood down from readiness,

"Tonight we celebrate!" After a bath and changing out of my sweaty flying suit, I was at the officers Kasino for dinner at 7:00 P.M. Jagdgeschwader 3 had links with the Henkell wine company, which ensured that the we never ran short of wine. Whenever a pilot was killed, it was usual for the Kommandeur to deliver a short requiem after dinner; then the pilots drank a toast to his memory before hurling their glasses (special cheap ones!) into the fireplace. But there had been no losses on this day.

The party would have gone on until after midnight, but it came to an end when

A wounded crewman is taken out the waist window of *Liberty Lib*, 458th Bomb Group, Horsham St. Faith, mid-1944. The Dodge ambulance doors are open, and there are more men yet to be offloaded. *USAF*

Mueller said, "Jungs, that's enough. We must be ready again tomorrow." At a Luftwaffe officers' party we did not have violent games. We sang songs (*not* Nazi party songs!): *"Es ist so wunder wunder schön, hoch in den blauen Luftigen Hohen"; "Oh, du schöner We-e-esterwald"; "Auf der Luneburger Heide, in den wunderschönen Land."* One of the officers would accompany the songs on a guitar. A pleasant comradely evening, with the officers steadily getting more and more drunk, then off to bed.

Bud Guillot
B-24 waist gunner, 392nd Bomb Group

You know, it's funny. You look back and you only remember the crazy things. Everything else just gets blacked out. There's always that moment, though, when for the first time in your life, you realize, "Someone is trying to kill me." It's a strange feeling. We were just kids—maybe eighteen to twenty-one years old. I've always heard people say, "If you're not afraid in combat, you're crazy!" I wasn't afraid in combat. My time was when I saw my name on the bulletin board, and I knew I was going to fly a mission the next day. It's hard to say why, but that's the way it was.

For example, the first time we flew through flak on the way to the target, I was sitting on some ammo cans watching the white puffs of 88mm flak come up. The first burst came away out in front of us and the next one was behind us. I said to myself, "Wow, this is going to be easy. These guys aren't very good." Well, little did I know they had just bracketed us. They had just zeroed

in on our altitude and direction. All hell broke loose below us and I never sat down on a mission again.

John Gabay
B-17 tail gunner, 94th Bomb Group

Munster, Germany, 11 November 1943 (ship number 846). It seemed at first to be a pretty easy mission. As we entered the Dutch coast we were met with light flak. Then our P-47s showed up, and we had no trouble at all until we reached the target. Flak wasn't too heavy, but our bomb bay doors wouldn't open. We finally got them open and got rid of the bombs in Germany. Our escort stayed with us as long as they could, engaging in several dogfights. They had to leave us over Holland and then the fun began.

About fifty Fw 190s and Me 109s attacked us from every direction. We couldn't close our bomb bay doors so they picked on us, thinking we were crippled. One Fw dove straight down from one o'clock high and let go with his cannons. He put a hole in our left wing big enough to crawl through. He also blew off a piece of the vertical stabilizer over my head. The Fort on our wing burst into flames and only five got out—one chute was on fire. They were from our barracks. A 109 came directly at me, and I know I hit him, as he rolled over in a dive and disappeared. Another one came in low at eight o'clock, and Chauncey, our ball gunner, hit him and he

When *5 Grand* (the 5,000th B-17 built by Boeing) went to war, it carried the company employees' autographs all the way to the 96th Bomb Group at Snetterton Heath. Here the B-17 makes a shakedown flight over England before getting painted with the group identification letter (square C), individual call letter (H), red vertical fin stripes on the tail, and squadron codes (BX) on the fuselage. *5 Grand* must have been a lucky ship; after seventy-eight missions, it went home to end up in the scrap yard. *USAF*

burst into flames and went down.

Several Fw 190s kept coming in at the tail, and I hit one. He rolled over, and I lost him. The Fort on our other wing burst into flames and went into a spin. Didn't see any chutes. Flak burst under our ship and concussion knocked us up about fifty feet. As we reached the Channel, an Fw 190 followed up low at five o'clock, and Chauncey knocked him into the water. We made it back OK, but our new ship was a wreck. This was our crew's first raid together.

Philip Ardery

B-24 squadron commander, 389th Bomb Group

I would like to correct a frequent fallacy made by writers describing bombing raids. The noise a bomber pilot hears is awful, but that noise isn't the loud noise of shells bursting. The pilot is encased in many thicknesses of clothing—even his head is almost completely covered. Tightly clamped against his ears are his headphones, built into his helmet. Out of these headphones comes most of the noise he hears. The horrible screaming is the noise of the radio-jamming apparatus of the enemy. It is like a death cry of the banshees of all the ages. On our missions it usually started faintly in our headphones as we neared the enemy coast and grew louder and louder. A pilot had to keep the volume of the receiver turned up high in order to hear commands over the air through the bedlam of jamming. After a few hours of it, I felt that I would go crazy if I didn't turn the volume down. I would turn it down when I was out of the target area, but I knew when I did that I might be missing an important radio order or a call from another ship asking for help or direction in one way or another.

We could hear the firing of our own guns. Chiefly we could hear the top turret. In addition to the noise of the top turret we could hear the nose guns, the waist guns, the ball turret, and finally the tail turret. We really couldn't hear the tail turret, but after we had ridden in our bombers for a while there was a peculiar faint vibration that would run down the skin of the ship and up the seats to let us know little Pete Peterson of Fowble's crew was warming up his guns. When Pete's guns chattered, some Nazi always regretted it. And when I felt the vibrations of his guns coming through the seat of my pants, it was like someone scratching a mosquito bite in the middle of my back.

But then about the flak. You could hear it—faintly. When flak was very near you could see the angry red fire as the shells exploded before the black smoke formed. You could hear the bursts sounding like *wuff, wuff, wuff* under your wings. You could see the nose of the ship plowing through the smoke clouds where the bursts had been. You could hear the sprinkle of slivers of shrapnel go through the sides of the ship if they were hitting close to you. I always said that if you hear the flak—if you get the *wuff, wuff, wuff*—and really hear it over the screaming of the radio and other sounds, then it is deadly close. You don't realize the terror it strikes into some airmen's hearts until you've had your own plane shot to hell a few times. I laughed at Franco's flak coming through Gibraltar. It wasn't much flak, but I wouldn't laugh six months later when I had seen more of it.

Sky marker smoke trails from the preceding formation drift beneath a 329th Squadron, 93rd Bomb Group Liberator heading for Ahrweiler, Germany, 24 December 1944. *Glenn A. Tessmer*

Friedrich Stehle
Me 410 pilot, II/ZG 26

If we attacked the bombers from behind, we could really work on them—if we were left alone by the enemy escorts. You really had to work on those bombers; it was very seldom that you knocked them down with the first burst. Sometimes you would sit behind a bomber and fire off all your ammunition into it, and it would not move. It would just keep going.

If you were attacked by a Mustang, you could only pray and hope your gunner shot well. I had a few tricks I could throw in, and perhaps they saved me. My Viennese gunner, Unteroffizier Alois Slaby, was very experienced, and he knew exactly when the enemy fighter was about to fire. He would say, "Not yet—not yet. Now!" and I would chop the throttles, and the 410 would decelerate very rapidly. If we were lucky, the fighter would go screaming past us. Sometimes I would put the 410 into a skid with the wings level, and the enemy rounds would flash past the wing tip. We knew that if we could buy a little time, that often meant survival. Once the escorts had dropped their tanks, they could not fight for very long near Berlin. They had to break off and return to England.

At 28,000 feet, the Me 410 was only just about flying. It could not maneuver much. Even at full throttle, we would be overtaking the enemy bombers at only about thirty miles per hour. As a result, it took us a long time to get ourselves into firing position. Fighting in the Me 410 was a bit like entering the Kentucky Derby on a cart horse!

149

By the end of the war, aircraft of the Eighth, Ninth, Twelfth, and Fifteenth Air Forces were operating over Germany. Though air superiority was a reality, Luftwaffe pilots continued to mount heavy opposition, particularly in the form of the jet-propelled Messerschmitt 262. This 320th Bomb Group B-26G got back to its French base with this damage from an Me 262's 30mm cannons. *Joseph S. Kingsbury*

John Gabay
B-17 tail gunner, 94th Bomb Group

Kiel, Germany, 13 December 1943 (ship number 846). Target: heart of city. We flew up through the North Sea and just as we entered the enemy coast, about forty Ju 88s appeared out of nowhere. They flew alongside our formation on both sides, but just out of range. After several minutes of this, they began to peel off, and four of them attacked our ship from the tail, one at a time. The flame from the cannons, tracers from their machine guns, and rockets from under their wings made the situation a bit hairy. All I could do, besides being scared, was to spray each one as they came in and call for evasive action.

I hit the second one, and he rolled over and burned. I saw my tracers slam into the cockpit of the third. I may have hit the pilot, as the ship started to go out of control. I poured more into it, knocking off the canopy under the nose. It looked like a leg hung out of the ship for an instant, then fell out. Then the ship went into a spin. More Ju 88s flew alongside of us, out of range. Some of them waved to us. It was shaky waiting for them to attack. Then they came at us. Our pilot used plenty of evasive action, and all guns were firing. The ball turret in the ship next to us was blown out. Several ships were hit hard. We had several flak holes, machine gun holes, and a couple of 20mm cannon holes in the right wing. A squadron of P-38s showed up for a change, and the bandits scattered.

One bomb got hung up in the bomb bay, but C. L. managed to dump it after a few

minutes. Leo was annoyed that I didn't put in any claims. I don't like the hassle. To-day—December *13;* Our Crew—*number 13;* bombs away at *1300.* Another lucky day.

Lowell Watts
B-17 pilot, 388th Bomb Group

Then the flak hit us. They didn't start out with wild shots and work in closer. The first salvo they sent up was right on us. We could hear the metal of our plane rend and tear as each volley exploded. The hits weren't direct. They were just far enough away so that they didn't take off a wing or the tail or blow the plane up. . . . they would just tear a ship half apart without complete-ly knocking it out. Big, ragged holes ap-peared in the wings and fuselage. The copi-lot was watching nothing but instruments, waiting for that telltale story on some in-strument that would indicate a damaged or ruined engine, but they kept up their steady roar, even as the ship rocked from the near-ness of the hundreds of flak bursts.

Missouri Mule **with the 320th Bomb Group over Dôle, France, 1945.** *Joseph S. Kingsbury*

Bombs away! The 320th Bomb Group bombs through clouds, 1945. They hit an eighty-five-foot rail bridge. *Joseph S. Kingsbury*

John Gabay
B-17 tail gunner, 94th Bomb Group

Bremen, Germany, 16 December 1943 (ship number 037). Target: docks—heart of the city. We were supposed to have plenty of escort—P-38s, P-51s, and P-47s, but we were late and missed them. When we saw the P-38s, they were passing us on their way home—not a nice feeling. Flak over the target was extra heavy. The sky was black with flak burst smoke, and I could smell it through my oxygen mask. The noise was cruel and the concussions were murderous. Every ship in the group must have had flak holes—we had plenty.

When we came out of the target area, the fighters were waiting for us. I never saw so many. They were hiding over the stale flak smoke. Our crew led the Eighth Air Force on this raid. We had two direct attacks at the tail, but they didn't press them. The low group in our wing got hit very hard. One of the Forts blew up. The Jerry that got him gave some exhibition of flying. He was something special. We had a British radar officer on board. His job was to confuse the German radar. It didn't work.

The weather over the Channel was bad and especially over our field. We made the landing on the first try but nearly collided with another Fort. There were two crack-ups later on. Our ship was a mess—full of holes. I thought the crew chief was going to cry. We were told at interrogation that Bremen put up more flak today than any city up to now. Big deal!

John Gabay
B-17 tail gunner, 94th Bomb Group

Brunswick, Germany, 10 February 1944 (ship number 498). Target: heart of city. I don't know how to start this one. I'm very tired. They told us at briefing the plan was to send 200 Forts deep into Germany as a decoy to lure up enemy fighters so our escort could try to knock out the Luftwaffe. It didn't turn out that way. As soon as we crossed the enemy coast, we ran into swarms of enemy fighters (at interrogation everyone agreed over 300 fighters at one time pounded our group). I knew we were really in trouble when about 150 of our escort showed up and immediately dropped their belly tanks so they could mix it up with the enemy. That meant they couldn't stay with us very long—and the raid was just beginning.

The Luftwaffe must have put up every fighter they had—Me 109s, 110s, 210s, 410s, Ju 87s, 88s, Fw 190s, and a new type of Focke-Wulf. We had '47s, '51s, and '38s. But

A bomber pilot's dream—a new Douglas A-26B Invader from the 416th Bomb Group, early 1945. The first Invaders entered combat with the Ninth Air Force on 19 November 1944. From the start, pilots knew they had a hot rod, with ten forward-firing .50-caliber guns, a bomb load of 4,000 pounds, and a top speed of 355 miles per hour. *Robert Astrella*

no Spits. Fighters hit us from every angle. I saw Forts and fighters blowing up, Forts and fighters going down smoking and burning, wings coming off, tails coming off, the sky full of parachutes, white and checkered. One guy floated into a low Fort—he was churned up by the propellers and took the Fort with him. It just rolled over into a dive. The sky was so full of tracers, 20mm cannon shells exploding, and even rockets. Steel was ripping into our ship with sickening sounds. There were times when I was afraid to shoot for fear of hitting one of our own planes or some poor guy in a parachute.

We were leading the high squadron of nine planes—only two of us got back. They attacked the tail four abreast and four deep, sixteen at a time. Their wing guns lit up like Luna Park. These guys were not fooling. There were countless dogfights. The P-47s at times were badly outnumbered, but they did a great job and stayed with us until the very last minute. A couple of them asked for a heading home and said they were sorry they had to leave, but they were very low on fuel. When they left, the fighters became even more aggressive—if that was possible. All guns were firing at the same time—the whole ship was vibrating. I was shooting at everything that came in range. I think I hit a few but was too busy to see what happened as another attack was already starting, then another, etc. I know Chauncey got an Fw 190. Ju 88s flew over us dropping aerial bombs, but they weren't effective. At one time there must have been 200 fighters above us in dogfights. I saw two P-47s go down, but I saw the '47s shoot down several Jerries.

The battle let up for about five minutes and about that time Chambers, our bombardier, called out large formations of fighters at twelve o'clock high. We all thought they were our escort coming in force from England to help. But it turned out to be Fw 190s and Me 109s—about 150 of them. Now the fun really began. We had no more escort. Forts and fighters were going down all

The 391st Bomb Group at Asch (Y-29), Belgium, April 1945. The A-26 had a fighter pilot's cockpit with one set of controls, all easily within reach—and it was light on the controls compared to almost any other bomber. Even though the Invader was only in combat for just over five months, it proved to be a very lethal ground-attack aircraft. *John Quincy via Stan Wyglendowski*

around us. Our ship got slammed with 20mm cannon and machine gun slugs—a miracle none of us were hit. At the end of the battle, twenty P-47s showed up and put up a magnificent battle. Flak over the target was heavy, but not bad on the way home. We made it back OK, but there are a lot of empty beds tonight. This old Fort really took a beating—I don't know how it stayed in the air. The damage: half the nose blown out; six feet of the vertical stabilizer blown off; tail cables severed; all my windows blown out; one 20mm went through left side of tail above my hands and blew up just outside my window. All in all, ground crew counted 136 holes.

John Gabay
B-17 tail gunner, 94th Bomb Group

Pas de Calais, France, 13 February 1944 (ship number 498). Target: rocket sites. We did squadron bombing today. Our crew led the low squadron. Each squadron had different targets. We flew over six or seven flak areas. Flak wasn't very heavy, but what they threw was right in there—medium to light but very accurate. It killed a navigator in our squadron. I didn't see any fighters—friendly or otherwise—on the way in, but I could hear every burst of flak. Maybe I'm thinking too much about flak. At least with fighters you can fight back. France looked so peaceful and quiet until bombs away. Forts were coming and going, dropping bombs on their own individual targets. I wondered what the heck was so important down there. The ground was covered with bomb bursts and once in a while a big explosion—a hit, I guess! One B-24 got hit bad by flak and flew in our formation all the way home. Coming back we saw some fighters near the Channel, but they ignored us. Thanks a lot.

John Flottorp
B-17 pilot, 390th Bomb Group

Engineering surveyed the damage and determined the aircraft beyond economical repairs. We had landed without brakes with the right tire burned badly after having to crank the gear down. Seventeen 20mm en-

try holes were counted along with numerous machine gun bullet holes and too many flak holes to count. The number three engine had the crankcase holed, the oil cooler shot away, a runaway prop, and a fire. The number four engine turbo waste gate had been hit and jammed in a partial power position. On one of the last attacks it had been hit again, and the top of one cylinder and valves were knocked out. Both numbers one and two had burned valves and pistons from overboosting and overheating but had held together. The bomb bay had been holed and the life raft compartment blown out. The vertical fin had collected seven 20mm hits that opened up the skin, looking like Swiss cheese the rats had been at, but the spar structure was not appreciably damaged. The main wing spar on the right wing had been virtually severed in two places along with the right aileron cables.

Each crew member had his own narrow escape. The tail gunner had a stoppage in one of his guns. He raised the armor plate and bent far forward to clear a jammed car-

tridge when a 20mm round slammed through from side to side where his head had been the instant before. It did not explode but left him a hole whistling by each ear. The waist and radio room had been sieved by flak and fighter fire, but no one got a scratch. The top turret gunner was firing at an attacking fighter at a high angle when a machine gun slug came through the turret Plexiglas, just missing his head. His helmet, goggles, and oxygen mask saved him from cuts from the Plexiglas fragments. The navigator, down in the nose, had his throat mike strap cut by a flak fragment leaving only a minor scratch on his neck.

We were just one crew who were inordinately lucky. The good Lord had other plans for us that day. The incredibly tough B-17 also deserves much credit.

Lowell Watts
B-17 pilot, 388th Bomb Group

I noticed the windshield and the top of the cockpit was gone, and I was sitting out in the gentle breezes. I could tell we rolled

With the A-26C came a clear plexiglass nose for a bombardier. The 386th Bomb Group gave up their beloved Marauders for these Invaders in St. Trond, Belgium, spring 1945. Within a very short time the group was sold on the new bomber. *Richard H. Denison*

A 386th Bomb Group A-26B over France, spring 1945. About the only real drawback to the new Invader was poor visibility to the side and down because the plane's engines extended forward of the cockpit. In the Marauder, the pilot sat far ahead of the engines,. *Richard H. Denison*

over upside down. My safety belt had been unbuckled so I fell away from the seat, but held myself in with the grasp I had on the control wheel. After a few weird sensations, I was pinned to the seat, unable to move or even raise my hand to pull off the throttles or try to cut the gas to the inboard engines. Flames now swept past my face, between my legs, and past my arms as though sucked by a giant vacuum.

John Gabay
B-17 tail gunner, 94th Bomb Group

February 9: Kersey and I got up to pre-flight at 4:00. Lieutenant Anderson and crew was to fly ours. As we got ready to start engines, the left waist gun went off—hit the tail gunner, who was outside, in the head. He was knocked down, and when we got to him, he was bleeding badly. We gave him first aid, and by then the ambulance came and took him away. I cleaned up the mess afterwards and found pieces of meat and brains. They operated on him and took out the shell casing that had pierced his skull. Luongo gave a pint of blood for transfusion. The doctor says he will live. This is the first time we've had an accident. The bullet was an incendiary that went through the door, then the trim tab on the elevator before it hit Millinger. Mission was scrubbed, so the damage was repaired today.

Ben Smith
B-17 radio operator, 303rd Bomb Group

We got out and looked her over. It was unbelievable. We had taken a savage mauling, and she was one more lacerated lady. That morning our bomber had been a lovely girl without blemish. The ground crews could do wonders with a shot-up B-17, but they had their work cut out for them with that one. Sometimes when one was shot up too badly, they made her a "hangar queen" and cannibalized parts off her. I remember the ground crew laid some rueful looks on us.

Bob DeGroat
B-24 pilot, POW Stalag Luft IIIA

It is sometime after midnight and pitch black. The air is humid and pungent, almost physically thick. I am accustomed to the smell, but if I had to describe it, I would say that it is equal parts of unwashed human/animal smells, masonry mildew, filthy ancient straw ticking, and unwashed clothing that has been worn every day for months. The lingering odors from Kriegie fat lamps, cooking devices fed from shaved bed boards, dried weed roots, or anything else short of rocks that can be found to burn are also evident.

As my eyes gradually become accustomed to the murk, I begin to make out the forms of the bunk blocks, four square and three tiers high. They are arranged in the familiar cubical pattern, allowing a wide aisle down the center of the barracks.

I become aware of a constant shuffle and passage of prisoners up and down the aisle, even at this hour. They represent the steady stream of men headed for the latrine that becomes a part of the Kriegie night life. When solid food is scarce, the addition of extra liquid helps to give a feeling of semi-fullness, but the penalty, of course, is paid in added trips to relieve the pressure. The diet in general affects various people differently. Some are in a situation of never-ending diarrhea; on the other hand, some find that if it's inconvenient to go today, just wait until tomorrow. But the liquid must be relieved on schedule, so I prepare to join the shuffling procession.

I am lucky. I have a top bunk. Although potentially the foul air rises, the roof is a good ten feet above me, and the air seems better up here. I also don't have any claustrophobia-causing bodies lying above me, and I don't have a constant number of groggy, semi-sleepwalkers climbing down over me to join the nightly procession to the "john."

I gently move my two three- by five-foot, threadbare blankets to the side. I grab my jacket . . . actually a Polish army coat that has been cut off at the waist and redesigned into a unique Eisenhower jacket. I carefully move to sit up. There are two reasons for moving with care. One is that if you sit up too suddenly, you might faint. The other and more important reason is that each of us is issued only three bed boards to support our thin straw mattress tick. I use one under my shoulders, another under my hips, and the third about at my calves. If I get any weight in the wrong place, there is a real danger of falling through into the bunk below. I swing my feet over and climb down to the floor, trying to avoid stepping on the hands and arms of my lower bunk mates.

I am dressed in my jacket, underpants, and shoes. It is a cool spring night out, and I'll be shivering by the time I return, but the barracks is almost hot with human-animal

The Twelfth Air Force's 320th Bomb Group marshaling for takeoff at Longvic, 1945. Unlike the heavy bomb groups of the Eighth and Fifteenth Air Forces, the Ninth and Twelfth Air Forces hopped from one base to another across Europe as the tactical battle lines moved. It was a gypsy's life with tents, mud, and dust being the norm.
Joseph S. Kingsbury

heat and I'll warm up quickly when I return. I try not to wear outer apparel to bed as there is almost no way to clean or wash anything, and it will have to last indefinitely.

Outside there are a few hooded lights, but the buildings stand out in long, low silhouette against the lighter sky. Directly ahead, at right angles to the row of barracks buildings, and well elevated on a manmade berm, is the latrine. It is really just a many-holed, brick outhouse and smells just as you would imagine. The Germans send the "honey wagon" around periodically in an effort to prevent overflow. I grope through the blackness to an available empty hole.

As I head back to the barracks, the fresh air is sharp. I can see my breath. I am shivering.

When I open the door, I have to pause to let my eyes adapt to the gloom, but also find that I'm almost subconsciously taking a deep breath before plunging into the thick,

overpowering atmosphere inside. I shuffle back to my bunk and climb up. I carefully arrange my body over the bed boards and drop off to sleep until the next latrine call. I average, like everyone else, about four times a night.

The entire barracks comes to life about 7:00 A.M. Prisoners are getting dressed, making conversation with bunk mates, or just puttering at unimportant things as only people who have no schedule and too much time on their hands can do.

At 8:00 comes "tea." This is kindly called "ersatz tea," but I have my suspicions that it is really water stained a bit with tree bark. It comes in a huge wooden tub lugged from the kitchen by four men using a carrying pole. It is placed in a convenient open spot in the barracks, and the appointed barracks rationer takes over. He uses an "official" instrument—a soup can wired to a stick handle.

The men in the barracks are organized into ten cubicles of twelve to eighteen men each. For purposes of food rationing, a meticulous log is kept, and the order of the cubicles is rotated at each issue so that the first becomes last and the last gradually works up to first. If there are any seconds left to be given out, they start exactly where they left off the last time; not just with the correct cubicle, but with the exact man within that cubicle.

I get in line with Cubicle No. 9, and shortly I am issued my Campbell's soup can ration of warm ersatz tea. I pour half into a cup for leisurely sipping; it is warm and tasteless, but it looks like tea. The other half I keep in my pot and use for a comfortable shave; it saves fuel needed to heat the water and is much better than a cold shave when your only blade is dull as a hoe.

About 9:00 A.M., when everything settles down again, it is time for *"Appell."* This is the first head count of the day. I join the formation in front of the barracks along with the rest of the men. Each of the six barracks within this compound has its own formation. When we are all formed, guards are sent through each barracks to check that they are empty. Then the numbers are laboriously counted, with a guard passing down both the front and back of each formation simultaneously to make sure no inmate changes position.

In the old days, in warmer weather, we made a game of being uncooperative, what we called "baiting the goon." The uniforms of the prisoners are so mixed and nonstandard that there is no longer any real attempt to keep the British separated from the Norwe-

gians, or the Poles, or us Americans. The best the guards can do is some kind of total count.

Return to the barracks is followed by the daily cleanup period. There is no official inspection, but cubicle leaders are constantly aware of the devastation that any contagion could bring, due to the tenuous resistance within the group. Floors are swept, beds are made, and on bright days, an attempt is made to air the area, clothing, and bedding.

With my chores done, I am free until noon. There's a couple of cold water sinks at the back of the barracks, and I find space there to rinse out my spare socks. They are about the only spares that I possess. That done, I hunt up a couple of bunk mates, and we go outside to get in our daily exercise walk. We are not preparing for the Olympics; we are just trying to slow down the deterioration. The rest of the morning is spent chatting in leisurely groups in the sunshine on the sheltered side of the building.

About noon, our wooden tub from the kitchen arrives for the second time. This time it is soup. The official story is that it is dehydrated vegetables, but for most of us it is simply "grass soup." I assemble with my cubicle in our proper order in line, and in due course, I receive my soup can allotment of grass soup. Today, on whim, I drain the liquid off and drink the bitter, rather evil-looking stuff in hopes that it has some nutritional value. Next, I take the grass part of the soup and, in my turn at the cubicle stove (ingeniously made out of crimped and bent tin cans from lush Red Cross parcel days), I fry the grass to a less limp state. It tastes different, if not much better.

Next page
The 458th Bomb Group crew of *Arise My Love and Come With Me* at Horsham St. Faith unfortunately lost part of their wonderful Varga calendar girl (January 1944) when additional armor plate was installed for the copilot. *USAF*

Now our bread ration arrives. I am the official cutter for cubicle number 9. The ration for our fifteen men today is a loaf and a half. A loaf is about the size of the average raisin bread loaf at today's supermarket, but it is very wet, very sour, very dark, and many times heavier. As I measure and estimate, trying to take every little bump and indentation into account, the rest of my cubicle mates watch me closely with a lot of shifting of weight from one foot to the other, but they do not say a word to interrupt my concentration. When I have finally arranged fifteen equal slices or lumps of bread (including crumbs) around the edge of the cubicle table and have noted a few heads nodding in agreement out of the corner of my eye, I ask for a volunteer. The volunteer turns his back to the table, and as I point at random to one of the piles, he gives a number between one and fifteen. I then number the piles clockwise consecutively from that number and point. Each man claims his ration, having gotten it as fairly and objectively as we can arrange.

Sometimes, at infrequent intervals, another ration occurs along with the bread. Several times we had four or five potatoes per man, each the size of a golf ball, though they were shot through with black spots and mostly rotten. We are not that lucky today.

At this point, the average Kriegie starts the long preparation of his "big" meal of the day, designed to coincide with the arrival of the evening tea ration. I am no different. Today I slowly and carefully whittle my precious bit of sour, dark bread into as many wafer-thin pieces as I can manage, while gobbling up the crumbs as they fall. Then,

with my time on the stove, I very carefully toast each piece lightly to drive out some of the wetness and hopefully some of the sourness as well. To boost my sagging morale, I go all out. I dig into my hoarded reserve for that little bit of German jam that I horse traded from a guard one day with a couple of the most valuable trading devices of World War II: the American cigarette. I coat each sliver with a fine film of jam—just enough to taste—and my banquet is ready. There seems to be something therapeutic about spreading both the preparation and the consuming of food over the greatest possible span of time, and I am prepared now to spread the act of eating almost nothing over the best part of the evening. I count success in strange ways these days.

About 5:00 P.M. we are called out for our second *"Appell."* I fall into my accustomed position in the formation out front and wait to be counted with the rest. This time there is a lot of explosive German shouting, excited gestures, and scurrying of guards through the barracks. Something has gotten screwed up in the head count. All I can do is wait. It could be someone has been removed for questioning, and the word did not get around. It could be just a bad count by the guards, or more likely, it is someone in a dark corner of the latrine, too miserable to get out for formation. Things finally get resolved.

Almost immediately upon return to the barracks, the evening "tea" arrives. Going through the usual ritual, I get my ration and take it along with my beautiful stack of jam-garnished wafers to a corner of the cubicle table. This is the best time of the day—the social time of the day. Lots of drawn-out conversation, lots of drawn-out eating. It is the best way to disguise the lack of bulk and calories in the diet.

Night falls, and this is the nervous time. We are waiting for the "bird." The bird is the almost nightly reading of the BBC news. One of the Norwegian prisoners has a crystal radio set contained in a wearable upper-tooth bridge (it can now be told). From this, our captured war correspondent (we have one in camp) makes up a news release for the camp. With the release complete, a reader will go from barracks to barracks and read the latest war news. At these times we have our own brand of security, with guards posted to prevent interruptions or discovery.

The news tonight is good. All European fronts are progressing. Of almost equal interest is the war in the Pacific and its developments.

Lights out is 9:00 P.M. Until that time, I wander outside for some fresh air and to discuss the bird with some others. Sometimes we are lucky enough to get in on an RAF bombing show to the north towards Berlin. Under those conditions, the guards try to force us all inside, but there is no show tonight.

At 9:30 the fat lamps are out, and conversation gradually dies out as well. I head for the cold water sinks and do what washing up I can. Back at the bunk, I remove my outer clothing and climb under my two meager blankets. I can hear a little movement here and there in the barracks, but most prisoners have learned to fall asleep easily. I will too.

CHAPTER 7

Little Friends

Clarence E. "Bud" Anderson
P-51 pilot, 357th Fighter Group

It seemed we were always outnumbered. We had more fighters than they did, but what mattered was how many they could put up in one area. They would concentrate in huge numbers, by the hundreds at times. They would assemble way up ahead, pick a section of the bomber formation, and then come in head on, their guns blazing, sometimes hitting the bombers below us before we knew what was happening.

In the distance, a red-and-black smear marked the spot where a B-17 and its ten men had been. Planes still bearing their bomb loads erupted and fell, trailing flame, streaking the sky, leaving gaps in the bomber formation that were quickly closed up. Through our headsets we could hear the war, working its way back toward us, coming straight at us at hundreds of miles per hour. The adrenaline began gushing, and I scanned the sky frantically, trying to pick out the fly speck against the horizon that might have been somebody coming to kill us, trying to see him before he saw me, looking, squinting, breathless.

Francis "Lefty" Grove
P-51 pilot, 4th Fighter Group

Nineteen October 1944, P-51 VF-T, FO number 1249A, Escort "Libs" to Mainz. On way home rounded up four B-24 stragglers and one B-17 and escorted them home. Made no note in my log book, but do remember one badly damaged B-24 kept calling for close escort. I remember sliding in close, and they kept calling closer, closer. Finally they said good—and I was between the tail and wing, flying formation. They said they'd keep their eyes peeled for bogies and tell me where. I could see the crew, and I hoped they weren't trigger happy—their voices were certainly not calm on the trip home. And fortunately we spotted no Huns. When we made landfall after crossing the Channel, I broke off and headed home. Another reminder—how grateful to be a fighter pilot.

Mid-summer 1944. One of the working checker-nosed Thunderbolts of the 78th Fighter Group based at Duxford, which was a Royal Air Force base "loaned" to the Americans. Airplanes in combat didn't last long. Dick Sharpe was lost in this one on a strafing mission to targets in the Netherlands area, 3 September 1944. The 78th was known for eight-ship line abreast takeoffs on the large grass expanse at Duxford, getting the entire group into the air in record time. *USAF*

John Gabay
B-17 tail gunner, 94th Bomb Group

When a red alert was on (that meant a raid the next day), we'd fill up the two tiny belly stoves with coal, put out the lights, and try to sleep. About 3:00 A.M., some guy would come in, switch on the lights, and scream out the names of the men going on the raid while ducking a few army shoes. We'd get dressed in about five minutes to keep from freezing, as the stoves were out and the barracks cold, damp, and miserable. We would file outside into the waiting truck amid mumbled gripes and curses.

The truck would take us to the mess hall for breakfast, then to the briefing room. (Before entering this room, you had to identify yourself to two MPs with machine guns.) We'd take our seats, and the usual chatter would be going on, but as soon as the briefing officer came on stage, the silence would be deafening. He would walk over to the large covered map in the center of the stage and pull the curtain off. If the line to the target was a long one, the moans and whistles filled the room. Then the briefing would begin. We didn't pay much attention to the weather report or the amount of flak batteries and fighters we would encounter along the way—these reports were always wrong. But we did pay attention to the length of the raid, the altitude, the type of bomb load, and most of all the escort. The few times we were to get the English Spitfire escort, the men would boo, but they would cheer whenever we would get Polish Spits. The English were very poor at escort duty—they never seemed to get the hang of it.

On one occasion, our group was getting shot up by about twenty Me 109s. A few minutes later twenty-seven British Spitfires showed up and half the German fighters

The ground crew of Lieutenant F. M. "Lefty" Grove's 4th Fighter Group P-51C Mustang get the aircraft ready for a morning mission, Debden, mid-1944. With the arrival of the Mustang came the range and capability the Eighth Air Force had needed since the very start of the bombing effort. With fighters able to go all the way to the target and back, the Luftwaffe was stopped in its tracks. *F. M. Grove*

A 48th Squadron, 14th Fighter Group P-38J Lightning on short final at Triolo, Italy, winter 1944–45. The P-38 had the range and firepower to make an excellent escort fighter, and it did a sterling job for the Ninth, Twelfth, and Fifteenth Air Forces. Unfortunately, it suffered from continual mechanical failures with the Eighth Air Force over Europe and was withdrawn in favor of the P-51. Lack of adequate cockpit heat was the most common complaint from pilots. *James M. Stitt, Jr.*

A 325th Fighter Group Mustang pulls up alongside a B-25 to provide some escort before breaking off for home base in Italy, fall 1944. The Mustang did well in all theaters of war. A pilot's airplane with an excellent cockpit, strapping into a '51 was like pulling on a pair of pants. *James M. Stitt, Jr.*

Fighter pilots—God bless 'em. First Lieutenant Bob Flynt and Captain Jim Stitt, 37th Squadron, 14th Fighter Group, Triolo, Italy, late 1944. The fighter boys always seemed to be without a care in the world, never lacked for girls, knew where the hooch was, and were so cocky that the bomber boys loved to hate them. All that didn't make a whisker's difference when a bomber was under attack by German fighters and a Little Friend showed up to keep the wolves at bay. *James M. Stitt, Jr.*

166

plowed into them and chased them, shooting down several Spits. Then the German fighters grouped up and continued to clobber us. It would not be fair to judge the Royal Air Force on these few incidents. They certainly proved themselves as great aerial fighters throughout the war, but they just weren't good at escorting American bomb-ers.

From the briefing room we went to see the chaplain, Father Joe Collins, and either got a blessing or went to group confession, then walked to the locker room and picked up our flight clothes and parachutes. Then to the squadron armament shack for our guns, which we checked out and cleaned thoroughly. Then we'd climb into the truck

There was no mistaking the 4th Fighter Group's Mustangs with their blazing red noses. Lieutenant Bob Dickmeyer's *Jan* rests in its sandbagged revetment on the outer perimeter of Debden. *Larry Hendel*

Freddie F. Ohr's 52nd Fighter Group P-51D *Marie* at Capodocino, Naples, November 1944, when the Mustang reigned supreme across Europe. *Fred E. Bamberger*

A 64th Squadron, 57th Fighter Group P-47D taxies in at Grosseto, Italy, December 1944. The Thunderbolt was equally at home escorting bombers or dropping bombs at close range. Its rugged construction and excellent Pratt & Whitney R-2800 engine made it one of the safer places to be in the air. *Fred E. Bamberger*

P-51Ds of the 364th Fighter Group running up for takeoff at Honington, August 1944. Each fighter carried two 110-gallon drop tanks, which added a good four hours' range at cruise power. This allowed the Mustang to roam Europe at will, a war-winning capability. *Mark Brown/USAFA*

and ride out to our plane where we would put in our guns (in the dark) and complete dressing. Then we would sit under the wings, smoke a cigarette, and wait for about five minutes for the officers to arrive. When they arrived there were always a few wise cracks; then the pilot would ask if everything was OK. If there were no problems, we would climb into the plane and wait for the signal flare to start the engines. At no time, from briefing until we were airborne, did we mention the target.

A 63rd Squadron, 56th Fighter Group P-47D taxies out at Boxted, mid-1944, with two 150-gallon drop tanks. At the normal cruise of 100 gallons per hour, this gave an extra three hours' flying time—absolutely essential to put the thirsty Thunderbolt deep into enemy territory. The 56th, unlike the other Eighth Air Force fighter outfits, decided to stay with its '47s rather than trade them in for Mustangs. *Mark Brown/USAFA*

A P-47D yet to be assigned to a line fighter group, pays a visit to Mt. Farm with a fresh set of theater markings and invasion stripes. The bubble canopy on later Thunderbolts gave pilots excellent all-round visibility, an absolutely crucial asset in air-to-air combat. *Robert Astrella*

A war-weary P-47D of the Eighth Air Force's Air Sea Rescue Squadron, later the 5th Emergency Rescue Squadron. Though the airplane has had some hard use, it has been retrofitted with a Malcolm Hood, an outstanding addition for searching at sea. From May 1944 through the end of the war, the rescue squadron devoted full time to rescuing pilots at sea. The '47s were fitted with droppable dinghies and sea markers and were a more than welcome sight for a guy floating in frigid water with nothing more than a Mae West. *Robert Astrella*

One of the most vexing of problems for Eighth Air Force planners was obtaining accurate weather information, particularly over the Continent. In April 1944, the 802nd Reconnaissance Group (P) was formed with reverse Lend-Lease Mosquito Mk. XVI bombers. The unit became the 25th Bomb Group (Recon) by August. These fast "Mossies", painted in PRU Blue with red tails (to keep friendly fighters from thinking they were Me 410s), were ideal to range ahead of the bomber stream, reporting weather and target strikes, taking photos of special areas, and (late in the war) dropping radar-blinding chaff ahead of the attacking formations. The happy pilots of these beautiful de Havilland all-wood wonders initially came from the almost forgotten P-38 pilots of the 50th Fighter Squadron who had been left in Iceland by the 14th Fighter Group since mid-1942 sitting boring alert. *Robert Astrella*

171

Hairless Joe, the P-47D Thunderbolt of legendary 56th Fighter Group ace David C. Schilling, who ended the war with twenty-two and one half air-to-air and ten and one half ground kills. With the group since it was formed in June 1941, Schilling was made commander of the 62nd Squadron, then group executive officer by August 1943. He began his string of victories with two kills on the 9 October 1943 mission to Emden. When group commanding officer Colonel Hubert "Hub" Zemke took over the 479th Fighter Group in August 1944, Schilling was given command of the 56th, a position he held until tranfering to the 65th Fighter Wing the next January. Aggressive and capable, Dave Schilling was one of the finest fighter pilots of World War II. *Robert Astrella*

The 339th Fighter Group flew in combat with the Eighth Air Force for just under a full year—30 April 1944 to 21 April 1945—and managed to score a total of 239.5 air-to-air and 440.5 ground kills, almost all under the command of one man, Colonel John B. Henry, Jr. This 504th Squadron Mustang

172

was an early P-51B in the group, originally Vern Blizzard's *Punkie*. When Duane Larson was assigned the aircraft, it was renamed *Swede* as a reflection of his family origins. *Robert Astrella*

A 22nd Squadron, 7th Photo Group P-51K taxies out on the eastern perimeter track at Mt. Farm, March 1945. After suffering a string of recce aircraft losses to German fighters, the group was assigned its own fighter escort, beginning January 1945, in the form of Mustangs. At this point in the war American industry was pouring out an almost unlimited supply of aircraft. *Robert Astrella*

When fighters had seen their day and managed to last through enough combat to be classified "war weary," they were usually herded off to some other form of useful service. This veteran P-47C from Atcham, Shrewsbury, early 1944, was with the 551st Fighter Training Squadron, where it introduced pilots fresh from the States to VIII Fighter Command tactics and doctrine. *Robert Astrella*

173

CHAPTER 8

Home

Richard Fitzhugh
B-17 pilot, 457th Bomb Group

After my combat tour, they sent me to a redeployment pool of some kind. I believe the name of the place was Stoke, a miserable-looking place, cold, with tarpaper shacks, in December during the Battle of the Bulge. News was very bad at that time. I somehow felt kind of bad about going home, so I called up my squadron commander and got him on the phone, and I told him that I was willing to come back and do some more flying if he needed me, because I'd heard over the radio or something that B-17s had landed all over the continent there. The whole Eighth Air Force was all over creation. He told me to leave well enough alone, so I caught a C-54 back to the States.

We stopped at the Azores, and an interesting thing I noticed there, while taxiing out, were the locals were eating out of the garbage cans of the kitchen. I'd never seen that before. Then Bermuda. Bermuda was spectacular. We flew at night and came in there in the morning. Beautiful, beautiful pink sand and blue water. I still have the newspaper-this was January 1945—*The Bermuda Gazette,* McKinley Field.

We landed at Washington National. This was an Air Transport Command C-54, and so we went through a processing line. When it got to my turn, the corporal sitting there says, "Are you married or single?" And I asked him what difference did that make? And he says, "Well, if you're single, you go to Atlantic City, New Jersey for R&R, but if you're married, you get to go to Miami Beach." It was snowing in Washington at that time. I'd been freezing to death for a long time in England, and I didn't want to go to Atlantic City, so I said, "I'm married." I really wasn't married. So he signs me up for Miami Beach. My mother was living in Washington at the time, so this was very convenient.

I went home, and first thing I did was call up Alice, my wife-to-be, and tell her that we had to get married in a hurry. She said, "When?" and I said, "Well, next week! I've got to be married before I report in to my

A stripped-down and slick B-26 Marauder on short final at Gablingen Airdrome near Augsburg, Germany, fall 1945. When everyone else went home, a few Americans were left as a part of the occupation forces, and life became pretty boring. This Marauder was "requisitioned" by the 355th Fighter Group as their "Whiskey Wagon," and it was sent on a number of important missions to bring back food and drink. It was ideal for fighter pilots used to fast cruising speeds. And the '26 could really go without the extra drag and weight of turrets, armor plate, and bombs. *Alexander C. Sloan*

This was the awesome, terrible price Germany paid for going to war: Münster, Germany, just after the surrender. Though controversy raged from the start over the effectiveness of American daylight bombing, no one argued against bombing as a crucial part of overall victory. *Mark Brown/USAFA*

The remains at the southwest end of Villacoublay Airfield, just outside Paris. This field came under continual bombing attack until the Germans finally retreated in mid-1944. Afterward, it was nearly impossible to clean up the damage and rebuild the hangars. Many years elapsed before the field was once again back to prewar civil standards. *Mark Brown/USAFA*

next station." So she said, "Well, I'll tell my mother." She agreed, but I'm not sure her mother did. She was working in Columbia, South Carolina, at the time, and her home was Manning, South Carolina. So I bought the rings, went on down to Columbia and got her. Of course, I didn't have a car; in fact, I didn't even know how to drive a car. I didn't have a driver's license. I finished a combat tour in the B-17, but I never learned to drive a car.

We took the bus to Manning, which was about, I guess, an hour away. Some of her friends had a car, but there were a bunch of them, and we couldn't all get in the car. Somebody bought the wedding cake in Columbia. You couldn't get a cake that size, I don't think, in Manning. So we had the cake, and, being an independent person, I said, "We'll take the bus, and we'll take the cake." So Alice and I got on the bus with the cake. She had a suitcase, I had a suitcase, and that's all we had.

The bus broke down after about thirty minutes, so the driver let everybody out on the highway. Here I am, standing there with my suitcase, a wife-to-be, and a cake. I'm out

there thumbing a ride to our own wedding! Then her friends came by, so we figured that we could really all get in there after all. I sat on somebody's lap, had the cake on my lap; and we all made it to the wedding. I don't think too many people have to hitchhike to their own wedding!

Bob Morgan
B-17 pilot, 91st Bomb Group

When General Eaker told us we could come back to the States as our twenty-sixth mission, we really didn't know what we were in for. All we knew was we were going home. We came back; we landed at Bradley Field, then flew on to Washington, D.C.'s National Airport as our first official stop. General Hap Arnold was there, and as we approached the field, through air traffic control he told us to buzz the field. Well, for Robert Morgan, that is a real license to steal. We did a pretty good buzz job. He also gave us full license during this three-month tour of the United States to buzz any place we wanted. So, needless to say, I had a good

Though they were glad to get out of combat and go home, few aircrews had any idea that their wonderful steeds of war would be discarded as so much scrap to be turned back into pots and pans . . . or to be simply broken apart, carted away, and buried. This forlorn B-26 Marauder at Herzogenaurach, Germany, is only a short time away from being chopped up, burned, and buried on the spot, late 1945. The work was given at minimal wages to local Germans, many of whom had been active fighter pilots. They were astonished at being paid by Americans for doing something they had tried so hard to do six months before. *Herbert R. Rutland, Jr.*

Heading home. A mixed bag of Forts from the 94th, 34th, and 490th Bomb Groups gather at Bury St. Edmunds after VE-day to fly back to the United States with as many servicemen aboard as can fit. Flying former combat aircraft back across the Atlantic was an ideal way to bring masses of former combat crews home without creating a massive tie-up of ships and transport aircraft. Afterwards the

177

aircraft were useless. Upon arrival in the United States, they were flown to one of many bone yards to await civilian buyers or the smelter's torch. *Byron Trent*

Altus, Oklahoma, August 1945. B-24s from the 459th Bomb Group, Fifteenth Air Force, and other units sit in the Midwest sun awaiting their fate. Virtually all of the aircraft were scrapped within a year or two. *Claude Porter*

Old Ironpants awaits its fate at Altus, Oklahoma, August 1945. The Liberator was not a favorite of civilian postwar buyers looking for usable aircraft. As a result, almost all the Liberators were scrapped, much to the heartbreak—or delight—of the pilots who flew them. *Claude Porter*

time—a real good time. Asheville is still talking about it! If you've ever been up there and seen the courthouse and city hall, we managed to get a wing between the two of them. This was a lot of fun, and we enjoyed it. I must say, though, that, at the end of the three months, I felt like I'd been through combat again. I was ready to go to the Pacific.

Jack Havener
B-26 pilot, 344th Bomb Group

"What a disgraceful way to go!" These were my words after watching a newsreel in March of 1946 showing the demolition of surplus B-26s at Landsburg, Germany. The camera stopped in front of one ship being stripped of equipment prior to the attachment of dynamite packs to the wing roots for separation from the fuselage. I recognized the airmen removing the radio gear as members of the 497th Bomb Squadron, 344th Bomb Group, as the camera panned to the left and showed the nose art name to be *Terre Haute Tornado*. Rising up in my seat, I exclaimed, "That's my ship!" and much to my wife's embarrassment, continued to moan, "Oh no—Oh no!" throughout the balance of the newsreel. Needless to say, I didn't enjoy the feature picture that followed. After flying in that aircraft for some thirteen months, it was quite a shock to see her pushed up into a scrap heap by a bull-dozer.

Bob DeGroat
B-24 pilot, 459th Bomb Group

People sometimes ask about my feelings concerning the civilian death and destruction our bombing caused. Although I was aware that this was undoubtedly happening, the fact that it was unintentional probably salved my conscience. All briefings were for military or industrial targets, and the view of destruction from 25,000 feet was usually a column of black smoke erupting through an undercast. I was also a bit hardened by the death and destruction I witnessed among the planes around me. It became an unemotional everyday job with attached personal risk.

Fred Weiner
POW, Stalag Luft VI

It didn't take long to get back into the life in America. Yeah, you wanted to get started, you wanted to be a part of civilian life. While I was still in uniform, I met Edith. I wanted to get married, to get a job—so it didn't take long to get going. There are some things that are hard to tell somebody about the fun we had in the prison camps. In order to go steady with me, Edith prom-ised to let her friends meet the guy before she got serious with him. We had a double date at the Paramount to see Frank Sinatra. So, don't ask—we're in a line and have to wait two hours to get in. We're talking, and it turns out the other guy was a POW at Stalag 17B. Here I was a POW from Stalag Luft

VI, so we started in with the stories—laughing and telling anecdotes about the prison camp life. Well, people gathered all around us to hear us talk. We could hear them in the background saying, "Didn't they say they were in a prison camp?"

Home! **What a sight for sore eyes in 1946 after several years overseas—Grand Central Station in Los Angeles. What a city in which to get off the train and get reacquainted with American life.** *Alexander C. Sloan*

Could there be a better place for a serviceman to find out that American girls were still the prettiest in the world than the beach at Playa del Rey, south of Los Angeles? Home at last. *James C. Leigh via Mrs. M. M. Leigh/ Jim Dietz*

Index